MICROSOFT® *Quick*

KU-048-574

MICROSOFT WINDOWS™ 3

Microsoft
P R E S S

KRIS JAMSA

PUBLISHED BY
Microsoft Press
A Division of Microsoft Corporation
One Microsoft Way
Redmond, Washington 98052-6399

Library of Congress Cataloging-in-Publication Data

Jamsa, Kris A.
    Windows 3 / Kris Jamsa.
       p. cm. -- (Microsoft quick reference.)
    Includes index.
    ISBN 1-55615-387-2 : $8.95 ($10.95 Can.)
    1. Microsoft Windows (Computer programs)   I. Title. II. Series.
QA76.76.W56J37 1991
005.4'3--dc20
                                         91-29840
                                       CIP
Printed and bound in the United States of America.

1 2 3 4 5 6 7 8 9 MLML 6 5 4 3 2 1

Distributed to the book trade in Canada by Macmillan of Canada, a division of Canada Publishing Corporation.

Distributed to the book trade outside the United States and Canada by Penguin Books Ltd.

Penguin Books Ltd., Harmondsworth, Middlesex, England
Penguin Books Australia Ltd., Ringwood, Victoria, Australia
Penguin Books N.Z. Ltd., 182-190 Wairau Road, Auckland 10, New Zealand

British Cataloging-in-Publication Data available.

Acquisitions Editor: Michael Halvorson
Manuscript Editor: Megan E. Sheppard
Technical Editor: Jim Fuchs

Contents

Introduction

In 1981, IBM released its first personal computer, Microsoft
released MS-DOS, and the PC revolution began. Throughout
the 1980s, millions of users learned to issue a variety of
DOS commands and to use a variety of applications.

By the end of the decade, most users had a word processor,
a spreadsheet, and possibly a database application they used
regularly. In fact, most users were seeking an easy way to
exchange information between applications—a method
that would eliminate the need to end one application before
looking up information stored by another.

In 1990, Microsoft introduced Windows 3.0, a program
designed to maximize productivity. Windows 3.0 made
computers easier to use, applications easier to learn, and
allowed several applications to run at the same time.
And—perhaps more importantly—it provided a simple
means of information exchange between applications.
Windows is a *graphical environment*: Its menus, icons
(meaningful symbols), and dialog boxes replace the often
cryptic commands that DOS requires.

Just as the 1980s saw the PC revolution, the 1990s are seeing
the Windows revolution.

How to Use This Book

This book is bursting at the bindings with information
you'll need to put Windows to use:

■ Part I defines the elements of a window and describes
how to use them with both a mouse and a keyboard. It
also introduces Windows' extensive online help feature,
which provides answers to your Windows questions.

■ Part II describes how to use the Windows Program Manager to execute applications. The Program Manager organizes applications into groups, simplifying the selection of related applications, such as a word processor and a spreadsheet. It also introduces the File Manager, which displays directory listings and performs essential file operations such as copy, rename, and delete. Part II also describes the Print Manager, which controls printer output, and the Task Manager, which moves you quickly among running applications.

■ Part III explains how to customize Windows according to hardware needs (printer types, port usage, memory, and network) and personal preference (window colors, keyboard speed, cursor blink rate, and so on).

■ Part IV introduces Windows' collection of *desktop accessories,* powerful programs that automate many of the items commonly found on your desk such as a clock, notepad, calculator, calendar, and appointment book.

Three appendixes provide you with special information:

■ Appendix A walks you through Windows installation.

■ Appendix B introduces Windows' special configuration files.

■ Appendix C provides an easy-to-read list of keyboard shortcuts used within Windows.

In short, this reference contains all the steps you need, not just to get Windows started, but to really put Windows to use.

PART I

Essential Windows Operations

This book assumes that Microsoft Windows is installed on your computer and that you're ready to start it and become acquainted with the basics of Windows. If Windows is not yet installed on your computer, you can get all the installation information you need by turning to Appendix A, "Installing Windows."

STARTING WINDOWS

To start Windows, type the following command at the DOS prompt (C:\>), pressing Enter as shown:

```
WIN <Enter>
```

The Windows *desktop*, similar to Figure 1-1, will appear on your screen. (If you get the message *Bad command or filename*, see Appendix A, "Installing Windows," for instructions on adding the Windows subdirectory to your computer's search path.)

Windows supports two kinds of windows: *application windows*, and subwindows within application windows called *group windows*. In Figure 1-1, Program Manager is an application window, and Main is a group window.

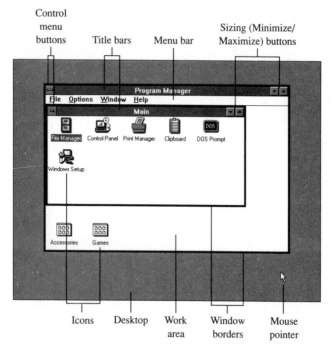

Control menu buttons · Title bars · Menu bar · Sizing (Minimize/Maximize) buttons

Icons · Desktop · Work area · Window borders · Mouse pointer

FIGURE 1-1. *After you start Windows, your screen will look something like this.*

WINDOWS AT A GLANCE

A *window* is simply a framed region on the screen. Each window contains the following elements (as shown in Figure 1-1):

- *Window borders* are the four edges that define the border of a window.

- The *title bar* is the area directly below the window's top border. The title bar displays the window's name.

- The *control-menu button* is the small box with an inner rectangle in the upper left corner of the window.

- *Sizing buttons (Minimize/Maximize)* are buttons in the upper right corner of the window that maximize or minimize the window.

- The *menu bar* is the area under the title bar. The menu bar provides access to most of an application's commands.

- The *work area* is the area inside a window.

- *Icons* are visual representations of minimized windows or applications.

Working with Icons

As shown in Figure 1-1, when you start Windows, you'll see a number of icons (graphical symbols of an application or a minimized window). To work with an icon, you expand it; that is, you cause the icon to become a window residing on the desktop.

To expand an icon, follow these steps:

Double-click on the icon.

For an application icon (an icon sitting on the desktop), repeatedly press Alt+Esc until the icon's name is selected, and then press Alt+Spacebar, R.

For an icon sitting within a group window, use the arrow keys to select the icon, and then press Enter.

For a group icon, repeatedly press Ctrl+F6 until the icon is selected, and then press Enter.

Working with Menus

Immediately below a window's title bar is a menu bar. The menu bar lists the names of one or more *menus* (lists of related commands). For example, the Program Manager menu bar contains the File, Options, Window, and Help menus.

Getting Around the Screen: A Primer

This book describes a variety of basic Windows operations. All can be carried out with a mouse or from the keyboard. (A mouse is strongly recommended, however.) The following symbols will help you find the instructions you need at a glance:

   Instructions for mouse users

   Instructions for keyboard users

In addition, mouse users should know how to perform the following actions. (Typical uses for these actions are noted in parentheses.)

To click
: Position the tip of the mouse pointer over the specified element, and then press and release the left mouse button one time. (Selecting windows, icons, or files in a list; selecting dialog box options.)

To double-click
: Position the tip of the mouse pointer over the specified element, and then press and release the left mouse button twice in quick succession. (Opening icons; executing applications; choosing items from a list.)

To drag
: Position the tip of the mouse pointer over the specified element, hold down the left mouse button, and move the mouse. The mouse pointer moves, dragging the element. Move the element to the desired location and release the left mouse button. (Moving windows or icons; resizing windows.)

Keyboard users should know how to use *keyboard shortcuts*. A keyboard shortcut is a single keystroke or a combination of keystrokes that execute a command directly. For example, the keyboard shortcut *Ctrl+F4* provides the same result as choosing Close from the Control menu of the Main window. Appendix C lists the keyboard shortcuts for a variety of tasks.

Opening a Menu

To open a menu, follow these steps:

 Click on the menu name.

1. For an application window, repeatedly press Alt+Esc until the window is selected.

   For a group window, repeatedly press Ctrl+F6 until the window is selected.

2. Press Alt+*X*, where *X* is the key that represents the desired menu name. (Each menu name has an underlined character that represents the menu. For example, press Alt+F to open the File menu.)

When you open a menu, you'll see a list of *menu items*, as shown in Figure 1-2.

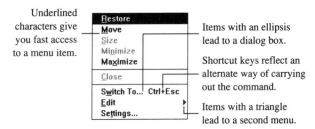

Underlined characters give you fast access to a menu item.

Items with an ellipsis lead to a dialog box.

Shortcut keys reflect an alternate way of carrying out the command.

Items with a triangle lead to a second menu.

FIGURE 1-2. *A sample open menu.*

Selecting a Menu Item

To select a menu item from an open menu, follow these steps:

 Click on the menu item.

 Press *X*, where *X* is the letter underlined in the menu item. If the menu item has no underlined letter, use the arrow keys to highlight the menu item, and then press Enter.

Closing a Menu

To close a menu without selecting a menu item, click on a location outside of the menu, or press the Esc key.

Working with Dialog Boxes

A *dialog box* is a window that frequently provides information and always requests a user response. Figure 1-3 shows a sample dialog box that helps you set up your printer. A dialog box might simply display a status message, waiting until you select OK, or it might ask you to specify a filename or other information.

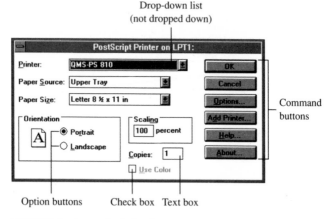

Drop-down list
(not dropped down)

Command
buttons

Option buttons   Check box   Text box

FIGURE 1-3. *A sample dialog box.*

Selecting a Dialog-box Field

Dialog boxes can contain several fields of information, as described in the following paragraphs. To select a field within a dialog box, follow these steps:

Click on the desired field.

Press Alt+*X*, where *X* is the letter underlined in the field name. Use the Tab key to advance forward from one dialog box field to the next. Use Shift+Tab to return to the previous field.

Command buttons — A command button directs a dialog box to perform a specific action.

Text box — A text box lets you type in a text string, such as a filename. Sometimes a text box contains default text (which might be highlighted). To enter different text, simply type in the new text. To make minor changes to the default text, press the left arrow key, and edit the text using the BackSpace, Del, and arrow keys.

List box — A list box provides you with a list of options. If the list contains more options than the box can display, the box will have a scroll bar. To select an option, follow these steps:

 Double-click on the option.

 Use the arrow keys to select the option, and then press Enter.

If the list lets you select multiple options, check the documentation that came with the application for instructions on selecting them.

Drop-down list — Dialog boxes use drop-down lists when there's not enough room for a list box. Figure 1-4 shows the sample dialog box with a drop-down list. To drop down the list, follow these steps:

 Click on the triangle at the right of the list.

 Select the drop-down list, and then press Alt+Down arrow.

Drop-down list
(dropped down)

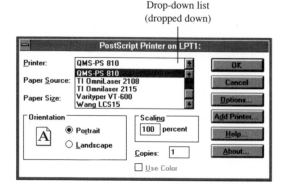

FIGURE 1-4. *A dialog box with a dropped-down list.*

Option button —When the options you can select from are
mutually exclusive—that is, when you are allowed to
select only one of them at a time—they are grouped
together as *option buttons*. Option buttons appear as circles
with text next to them. One option in each group—the
currently selected option—has a darkened circle. Gray or
dimmed options are inappropriate for the current situation
and cannot be selected.

To select an option button, follow these steps:

      Click on the option button.

      Press Alt+*X*, where *X* is the letter underlined in
the option name. If the option name doesn't have
an underlined letter, press the Tab key until one
of the options is encircled by a dotted line. Use
the arrow keys to move the darkened circle to the
desired option, and then press Enter.

Check box —Options that can be individually turned on
or off are displayed as check boxes. When a check box is
empty, the option is off. An X in the check box indicates
that the option is selected. Gray or dimmed options are inappropriate for the current situation and cannot be selected.

To select or deselect a check box, follow these steps:

 Click on the check box.

 Press Alt+*X*, where *X* is the letter underlined in the check box name. If the check box name doesn't have an underlined letter, press the Tab key until the option is encircled by a dotted line, and then press the Spacebar.

Scrolling for Information

When a Windows application contains more information than can fit in a window, you'll see vertical and horizontal scroll bars along the window's right and bottom edges, as shown in Figure 1-5. Mouse users can use these scroll bars to scroll through an entire document. (Keyboard users simply use the PgUp, PgDn, and arrow keys to scroll.) Within the scroll bars, a *scroll box* moves to reflect your relative position within the document.

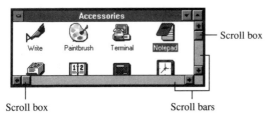

Scroll box

Scroll box   Scroll bars

FIGURE 1-5. *Scroll bars and scroll boxes help you work within your document.*

To use scroll bars, follow these steps:

- To move a short distance, click on the up and down or left and right arrows at each end of the scroll bar.
- To move up by approximately one screen, click on the scroll bar above the scroll box. To move down by approximately one screen, click on the scroll bar below the scroll box.

■ To move to a specific location, drag the scroll box along the scroll bar to quickly scan through the window's contents.

 Use the arrow keys or the PgUp and PgDn keys to scroll through the window's contents.

Sizing a Window

Windows provides you with several ways to increase and decrease the size of a window.

Minimizing a Window

To minimize a window—that is, to reduce it to an icon— follow these steps:

 Click on the Minimize button in the upper right corner of the window.

 For an application window, repeatedly press Alt+Esc until the window is selected (that is, until the borders darken), and then press ·Alt+Spacebar, N.

For a group window, repeatedly press Ctrl+F6 until the window is selected, and then press Alt+Hyphen, N.

Restoring a Minimized Window

To restore a minimized window—that is, to expand an icon to a window—follow these steps:

 Double-click on the icon.

 For an icon on the desktop, repeatedly press Alt+Esc until the icon is selected, and then press Alt+Spacebar, R.

For a group icon, repeatedly press Ctrl+F6 until the icon is highlighted, and then press Alt+Hyphen, R.

Maximizing a Window

To maximize a window—that is, to enlarge it to use the entire screen—follow these steps:

 Click on the Maximize button in the upper right corner of the window.

 For an application window, repeatedly press Alt+Esc until the window is selected, and then press Alt+Spacebar, X.

For a group window, repeatedly press Ctrl+F6 until the window is selected, and then press Alt+Hyphen, X.

Restoring a Maximized Window

When you maximize a window, that window's Maximize button becomes a Restore button. To restore a window to its previous size, follow these steps:

 Click on the Restore button.

 For an application window, repeatedly press Alt+Esc until the window is selected, and then press Alt+Spacebar, R.

For a group window, repeatedly press Ctrl+F6 until the window is selected, and then press Alt+Hyphen, R.

Incrementally Sizing a Window

To stretch or compress a window, follow these steps:

 Drag a window border to the desired size. When you release the mouse button, Windows expands or shrinks the window to fill the new area.

- To change window height, drag a horizontal border.

- To change window width, drag a vertical border.

■ To change both height and width, drag a corner of two borders.

1. For an application window, repeatedly press
   Alt+Esc until the window is selected, and then
   press Alt+Spacebar, S.

   For a group window, repeatedly press Ctrl+F6
   until the window is selected, and then press
   Alt+Hyphen, S.

2. Press the arrow key that corresponds to the
   window border you want to change. The up
   arrow key corresponds to the top border, the
   down arrow key corresponds to the bottom
   border, the right arrow key corresponds to the
   right border, and the left arrow key corresponds to the left border. (To change both
   height and width at the same time, press two
   arrow keys simultaneously.)

3. Using the arrow keys, move the border to the
   desired location and press Enter. When you
   press Enter, Windows expands or shrinks the
   window to fill the new area.

Moving a Window

One of the benefits of the Windows desktop is that it allows
you to move your work around to suit your needs and
priorities. To move a window, follow these steps:

Drag the title bar of the window—or drag the
icon—to the desired location.

1. For an application window, repeatedly press
   Alt+Esc until the window is selected, and then
   press Alt+Spacebar, M.

   For a group window, repeatedly press Ctrl+F6
   until the window is selected, and then press
   Alt+Hyphen, M.

2. Use the arrow keys to move the window to the
   desired location, and then press Enter.

NOTE: *When you move a window, Windows moves only an outline of the window until you release the mouse button or press Enter.*

Using the Control Menu

Every window has a *Control menu*, which contains commands that let you move, size, or close a window by using the keyboard (Figure 1-6). To open the Control menu, follow these steps:

 Click on the Control menu button in the window's upper left corner adjacent to the menu bar.

 For an application window, press Alt+Spacebar. For a group window, press Alt+Hyphen.

FIGURE 1-6. *A typical Control menu.*

The following list briefly describes each Control menu item:

Menu Item	Function
Restore	Restores a window to its previous size following a minimize or maximize operation
Move	Lets you move the window using the keyboard
Size	Lets you change the window's size using the keyboard
Minimize	Reduces the window to an icon
Maximize	Expands the window to full size
Close	Closes the window
Switch To	Selects the Task List, which lets you select another running application
Next	Selects the next open group window within an application window

Selecting a Window

When your screen contains several application windows, you can select the one you want by clicking on the window or by repeatedly pressing Alt+Esc. You can tell when a window is selected: Its borders and menu bar darken.

Closing a Window

When you close an application window, the corresponding application stops. If you have made changes and have not yet saved the changes on disk, a dialog box will appear asking whether you want to save the changes.

To close a window, follow these steps:

 Double-click on the window's Control menu button.

 For an application window, press Alt+Spacebar, C. For a group window, press Alt+Hyphen, C.

IF YOU NEED HELP

To help you quickly resolve problems and to answer your questions, Windows provides online help that you can use from within Windows. Simply use one of the following techniques:

■ Make a selection from the Help menu on the menu bar.

■ Press F1 while working within an application window.

■ Select Help from a dialog box.

The following list describes the Help menu items provided by most applications:

Item	Contents
Keyboard	Keyboard shortcuts the application supports
Commands	Description of each of the applications menu items
Procedures	Step-by-step instructions for performing specific tasks

When you select an item from the Help menu or when you press F1, you'll see a window with help text and the following buttons (Figure 1-7). (Dimmed buttons are inappropriate for the current situation and cannot be selected.)

To select a help button, follow these steps:

    Click on the help button.

    Press Alt+*X*, where *X* is the letter underlined in the button name.

Displays the help index

Displays the previous help text

Displays the previous topic in a series

Displays the next topic in a series

Lets you select a topic based on a keyword search

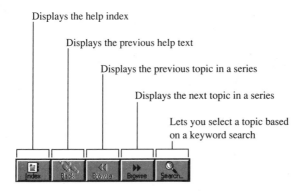

FIGURE 1-7. *The help buttons.*

Accessing Expanded Help

Additional information is available for terms that are underlined in the help text. To obtain additional information, follow these steps:

    Click on the underlined term.

    Press the Tab key to highlight the term, and then press Enter.

Accessing Definitions

Definitions are available for terms that have a dotted underline in the help text. To see the definition of the word, follow these steps:

 Click on the keyword.

 Press the Tab key to highlight the keyword, and then hold down the Enter key.

Exiting Online Help

To exit the online help, double-click on the help window's Control button, or press Alt+F4.

Printing a Help Topic

To print the help topic, choose Print from Help's File menu.

Performing a Keyword Search

The Search button lets you search for help from a list of predefined keywords. To choose the Search button, click on the Search button, or press Alt+S.

When you choose the Search button, you'll see a dialog box similar to Figure 1-8:

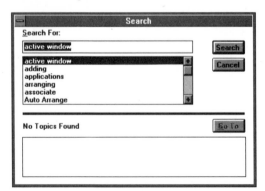

FIGURE 1-8. *The Search dialog box.*

The Search For list box contains the available keywords; the Topics Found list box will display the results of your search.

1. Select a keyword from the list box. (In addition to scrolling in the typical way, you can type the first letter or two of the desired keyword, and the cursor will move to the first keyword that matches the letters you specified.)

2. If you find the desired keyword, choose Search. Help searches the help file for matching occurrences of the keyword and displays each match in the Topics Found list box.

3. If a reference in the Topics Found list box is of interest, double-click on the reference, or use the arrow keys to select it, and then press Enter.

Bookmarks

To help you learn efficiently as well as effectively, Windows provides a bookmark command that lets you mark your place in Help before you exit. Later—rather than browsing to find where you left off—you can return directly to the place you marked.

Defining a Bookmark

To define a bookmark, follow these steps:

1. Choose Define from Help's Bookmark menu, or press Alt+M, D. You'll see the Bookmark Define dialog box, which contains the current help topic as the bookmark name (Figure 1-9).

2. Choose OK to accept the current name, or edit the name to your liking, and then choose OK to store the bookmark.

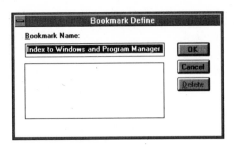

FIGURE 1-9. *The Bookmark Define dialog box.*

Accessing a Bookmark

To return to a marked position, follow these steps:

1. Choose Bookmark from the Help menu. You'll see a numbered list of every bookmark you've defined. (These lists appear underneath the Define menu item.)

2. Click on the desired bookmark, or press the number that corresponds to the desired bookmark. You can also highlight the bookmark with the arrow keys and press Enter.

Deleting a Bookmark

To delete a bookmark, follow these steps:

1. Choose Bookmark from the Help menu.

2. Choose Define.

3. Select the bookmark you want to delete.

4. Choose Delete.

EXITING WINDOWS

To exit Windows, follow these steps:

1. Close all open application windows, saving open files as necessary.

2. Choose Exit from the File menu. The Exit Windows dialog box appears (Figure 1-10), confirming that you want to exit.

FIGURE 1-10. *The Exit Windows dialog box.*

3. Select Save Changes if you want to save the current arrangement of your desktop.

4. Choose OK.

PART II
Standard Windows Applications

There are several key Windows applications you'll be
using: the Program Manager, the File Manager, the Print
Manager, and the Task List. In this section, you'll learn
about each of them.

THE PROGRAM MANAGER

The most important Windows application is the *Program
Manager.* The Program Manager is the window from which
you start your applications. (See Figure 2-1.)

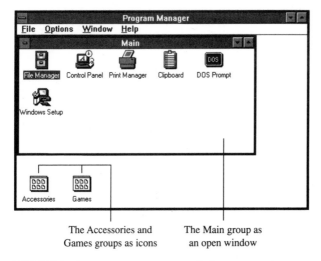

    The Accessories and   The Main group as
    Games groups as icons   an open window

FIGURE 2-1. *A group can appear as a window or as an icon.*

The Program Manager organizes applications into *groups*. A group can appear as an open window (*group window*) or as a minimized icon, as shown in Figure 2-1. A group window is considered a subwindow of the Program Manager. Three groups—Main, Accessories, and Games—are standard Windows:

Group	Contents
Main	Applications that let you configure your hardware and customize the Windows environment
Accessories	Applications that automate desktop tasks (clock, calculator, notepad, and calendar)
Games	The games Reversi and Solitaire

You might also have a Windows Applications group and a Non-Windows Applications group:

Group	Contents
Windows Applications	Applications specifically designed for Windows
Non-Windows Applications	DOS applications

Temporarily Exiting Windows to DOS

If you need to leave Windows temporarily and go to DOS, you can do so easily by choosing the DOS prompt icon from the Main group. When you return to Windows, your previously open windows and files will remain unchanged. To return to Windows from DOS, use the Exit command as shown here:

```
C:\>EXIT
```

When you go to DOS, do not turn off your computer without first returning to Windows and closing any applications that are running. This assures that all files are saved correctly.

Adding a Program Group

To help you organize your work effectively, the Program Manager lets you create your own groups. For example, you might create a group called Business, which might contain a spreadsheet, a word processor, and a project scheduler. To create a group, follow these steps:

1. Choose New from the Program Manager's File menu. You'll see the dialog box shown in Figure 2-2.

FIGURE 2-2. *The New Program Object dialog box.*

2. Select Program Group, and choose OK. You'll see the dialog box shown in Figure 2-3.

FIGURE 2-3. *The Program Group Properties dialog box.*

3. Type in the description you want to appear in this group window's title bar. Click OK or press Enter.

Deleting a Program Group

If you decide a group is no longer necessary, you can delete it by following these steps:

1. Minimize and select the group you intend to delete.

2. Choose Delete from the File menu, or press the Del key. You'll see a dialog box similar to the one shown in Figure 2-4.

FIGURE 2-4. *The Delete dialog box.*

3. If the dialog box displays the correct group name, choose Yes; otherwise, choose No.

Adding Applications to a Group

After you create a group, you will want to add applications to it. Likewise, if you buy a new application that runs under Windows (such as Word for Windows), you will want to add the application to the Windows Applications group. To add an application to a group, follow these steps:

1. Select the desired group window.

2. Choose New from the File menu. You'll see the New Program Object dialog box (Figure 2-2).

3. Select Program Item, and choose OK. You'll see the dialog box shown in Figure 2-5.

FIGURE 2-5. *The Program Item Properties dialog box.*

4. Type in the description you want to appear beneath the application's icon. Do *not* press Enter.

5. Move to the Command Line field. Type in the application's complete filename, including the drive letter, pathname, and filename extension. Choose OK.

Deleting Applications from a Group

To delete an application from a group, follow these steps:

1. Select the icon of the application you want to delete.

2. Choose Delete from the File menu, or press the Del key.
   You'll see a dialog box similar to the one shown in
   Figure 2-6.

FIGURE 2-6. *The Delete dialog box.*

3. If the item specified is the application you want to delete, choose Yes; otherwise, choose No.

Moving an Application
from One Group to Another

To move an application from one group to another, follow
these steps:

Hold down Ctrl key, and drag the application's
icon into the desired group window or atop the
desired group icon.

1. Select the icon of the application you want to
   move.

2. Choose Move from the File menu. You'll see a
   dialog box similar to the one shown in Figure
   2-7.

FIGURE 2-7. *The Move Program Item dialog box.*

3. Select the group to which you want the application moved. Choose OK.

Copying an Application from One Group to Another

To copy an application from one group to another, follow these steps:

Hold down the Ctrl key, and then drag the application's icon into the desired group window or atop the desired group icon.

1. Select the icon of the application you want to copy.

2. Choose Copy from the File menu. You'll see a dialog box similar to the one shown in Figure 2-8.

FIGURE 2-8. *The Copy Program Item dialog box.*

3. Select the group to which you want the application copied. Choose OK.

Changing a Group Name

To change the name of a group, follow these steps:

1. Minimize and then select the desired group's window.

2. Choose Properties from the File menu. You'll see a dialog box similar to the one shown in Figure 2-9.

FIGURE 2-9. *The Program Group Properties dialog box.*

3. Type a new group name in the Description field, and choose OK.

Changing an Application's Description

To change an application's description, follow these steps:

1. Select the application's icon.

2. Choose Properties from the File menu. You'll see a dialog box similar to the one shown in Figure 2-10.

FIGURE 2-10. *The Program Item Properties dialog box.*

3. Type in the new description. Choose OK.

Tiling or Cascading Group Windows

The Program Manager Window menu has two menu items that help you view group windows. The first, Cascade, arranges group windows one on top of another. The second, Tile, changes the size and position of each group window so that each is fully visible.

To arrange windows to best suit your needs, choose either Cascade or Tile from the Window menu.

Arranging Application and Group Icons

As you work with Windows, icons sometimes become disorganized within a group window. To tidy up the arrangement of icons, follow these steps:

1. Select the group window whose icons you want to arrange.

2. Choose Arrange Icons from the Window menu.

As you change the size of a group window, Windows might need to rearrange the icons so you can view them. Choose

Auto Arrange from the Options menu to have Windows automatically rearrange a resized group window's icons.

THE FILE MANAGER

The File Manager is a powerful application that lets you copy, delete, print, and rename files, run applications, and even perform disk operations such as formatting a new floppy disk.

When you start the File Manager, you'll see a screen similar to the one in Figure 2-11.

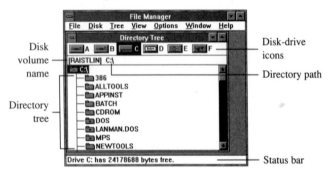

FIGURE 2-11. *Your screen will look like this after you start the File Manager.*

■ *Disk-drive icons* represent the drives available to the File Manager. Drives are of the following types: floppy-disk drive, hard-disk drive, network drive, RAM drive, and CD-ROM drive.

■ The *disk volume name* is an optional 11-character name you can assign to your disk. (If your disk is unnamed, this field does not appear.)

- The *directory path* shows the full pathname to the current directory.

- The *directory tree* displays directories of the current drive. Directories that contain additional subdirectories are shown with a plus sign (+) inside the directory's icon.

- The *status bar* displays the amount of free space the current drive contains.

Fundamental File Manager Operations

This section describes how to

- Change drives
- Expand and collapse directories
- Open and close directory windows
- Run applications

Changing Drives

You can change to any drive represented by a drive icon. To change to a drive, click on the drive's icon, or press Ctrl+*X*, where *X* is the letter of the desired drive.

Expanding Directories

DOS lets you store files in *directories*. Directories are organizational tools that allow you to group related files together. Think of a directory as a folder inside a filing cabinet.

Directories can also contain other directories. A directory that contains another is called a *parent directory*. A directory within another is called a *subdirectory*.

The File Manager displays the contents of the current disk. Directories are displayed as icons that look like folders. (See Figure 2-11.) If a directory contains one or more subdirectories, its icon will contain a plus sign. To see these subdirectories, follow the steps below.

Expanding a Single Directory

To expand the subdirectories of a directory, click on the plus sign in the directory's icon, or select the directory's icon and press +.

The File Manager expands the directory, showing its subdirectories and replacing the plus sign in the directory's icon with a minus sign.

To expand the directory to show all its subdirectories, including subdirectories within subdirectories, follow these steps:

1. Select the desired directory.

2. Choose Expand Branch from the Tree menu, or press the asterisk (*) key.

Expanding the Entire Tree

To expand all directories on the current disk, choose Expand All from the Tree menu, or press Ctrl+*.

Collapsing a Directory

By *collapsing* a directory, you hide its subdirectories. To collapse a directory, follow these steps:

 Click on the minus sign inside the directory's icon.

 Select the directory, and then press –.

Opening and Closing Directory Windows

Expanding a directory reveals only subdirectory names. To view the files within a directory, you must open a *directory window*. (This is similar to changing the current directory at the DOS prompt.)

Opening a Directory Window

To open a directory window, choose the directory name. You'll see a window similar to Figure 2-12.

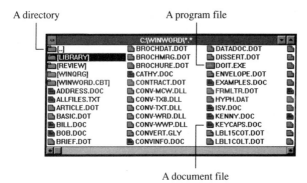

A directory   A program file

A document file

——— A directory

——— A program file

——— A document file

FIGURE 2-12. *An open directory window.*

Organizing Directory Windows

Each time you open a directory window from a directory window, the File Manager—by default—places the new window in front of the existing window. You can, however, choose to have a new directory window *replace* the existing one. To do so, choose Replace on Open from the View menu.

The icon appearing next to each filename indicates the file's type: a directory file, a program file (a COM, EXE, BAT, or PIF file), or a document file created with an application. When you choose a document file, Windows runs the corresponding application and loads the chosen document into the application.

Closing a Directory Window

To close a directory window, follow these steps:

 Double-click on the window's Control menu button.

 Choose the Close option from the window's Control menu, or press Ctrl+F4.

Running Applications

When you open a directory window, the File Manager displays the files the directory contains. From this list of files, you can run applications and work with files.

The File Manager provides several ways to run an application.

■ If the application's name appears in the directory window, you can double-click on or choose the application's name.

■ If the application's name does not appear in the directory window, follow these steps:

1. Choose Run from the File menu. You'll see a dialog box similar to the one in Figure 2-13.

![Run dialog box showing Current directory is C:\WINDOWS, Command Line field, Run Minimized checkbox, OK and Cancel buttons]

FIGURE 2-13. *The Run dialog box.*

2. Type in the name of the application you want to run, along with any additional information the application requires.

3. Select the Run Minimized box if you want the application to run in the background as an icon. Choose OK.

Changing the File Information Displayed

By default, the File Manager displays only filenames and extensions. You can display other file characteristics by making selections from the View menu.

Seeing File Details

To display each file's name, extension, size, date/time stamps, and file attributes, choose File Details from the View menu. To hide these attributes, choose Name from the View menu.

Customizing Directory Window Information

To have specific file information appear in the directory window, follow these steps:

1. Choose Other from the View menu. You'll see a dialog box similar to the one in Figure 2-14.

FIGURE 2-14. *The View Other dialog box.*

2. Select the file details you want the File Manager to display.

NOTE: *Select Set System Default if you want the File Manager to display these details in each directory window you open. Otherwise, file details are shown only in the current window.*

3. Press Enter or choose OK.

Changing the Order of Directory Window Contents

Within a directory window, you'll see a list of directories followed by a list of filenames. Both the directory and file-name lists are sorted in alphabetic order. You can sort by other file details, however, by choosing Sort by from the View menu.

Using Sort By

To sort by other file details, follow these steps:

Selecting Multiple Files

When you need to select more than one file, you can use one of several methods, depending on how the files are arranged in the directory.

Selecting Consecutive Files

To select files whose names appear consecutively in the directory window, follow these steps:

 Click on the first filename in the group. Hold down the Shift key, and click on the last filename in the group.

 Select the first file in the group. Hold down the Shift key, and use the arrow keys to select the remaining files in the group.

Selecting Nonconsecutive Files

To select multiple files whose names are not consecutive, follow these steps:

 Hold down the Ctrl key, and click on each file-name desired.

 1. Press Shift+F8. The cursor frame will begin to blink.

1. Choose Sort by from the View menu. You'll see a dialog box similar to the one in Figure 2-15.

FIGURE 2-15. *The Sort By dialog box.*

2. Use your arrow keys and the Spacebar to select each desired file.

3. After you've selected all desired files, press Shift+F8.

Selecting All Files

To select all the files in the directory, choose Select All from the File menu, or press Ctrl+/.

Canceling a Selection

To cancel a selection, follow these steps:

Hold down the Ctrl key, and click on the file to deselect.

1. Press Shift+F8. The cursor frame will begin to blink.

2. Use the arrow keys to move to the file you want to deselect. Press the Spacebar.

3. Press Shift+F8.

Canceling All Selections

To cancel all file selections, choose Deselect All from the File menu, or press Ctrl+\.

2. Select the desired sort detail.

NOTE: *Check the Set System Default box if you want the File Manager to use this file detail to sort every window you open. Otherwise, the sort detail applies only to the current window.*

3. Press Enter or choose OK.

Restricting the File Types Displayed

By default, a directory window displays the name of every type of file in the directory. To restrict which file types appear, follow these steps:

1. Choose Include from the View menu. You'll see a dialog box similar to the one in Figure 2-16.

FIGURE 2-16. *The Include dialog box.*

2. Select those file types you want the File Manager to display.

NOTE: *Check the Set System Default box if you want the File Manager to display these file types in each window. Otherwise, the selection applies only to the current window.*

3. Press Enter or choose OK.

Using the File Menu

The File menu performs a variety of tasks, such as renaming and copying files. Figure 2-17 briefly describes each File menu item.

Menu Item	Function
Open	Opens a directory window, runs the application, or runs the application that created the selected document and loads the document into the application
Run	Runs an application
Print	Prints one or more files
Associate	Associates a file type with an application
Search	Searches the current disk for a file
Move	Moves one or more files to a different disk or directory
Copy	Copies one or more files to a different disk or directory
Delete	Deletes one or more files or directories
Rename	Renames one or more files
Change Attributes	Assigns new file attributes to one or more files
Create Directory	Creates a directory
Select All	Selects all files in the directory window
Deselect All	Deselects all files in the directory window
Exit	Stops the File Manager

FIGURE 2-17. *File menu descriptions.*

Printing Files

To print one or more files, follow these steps:

1. Select the file or files you want to print.

2. Choose Print from the File menu. You'll see a dialog box similar to the one in Figure 2-18.

FIGURE 2-18. *The Print dialog box.*

3. Choose OK.

Associating Files

Every document file created with a Windows application has a *filename extension*. (For example, every Word for Windows document file has the DOC filename extension.) This extension—the characters at the end of the file-name—can be used to associate all files that end in that extension with an application.

By using Associate from the File menu, you can have Windows run the associated application—and load the selected file—each time you select a file with a particular file extension. (For example, by simply selecting any file with the DOC extension, you'd trigger Word for Windows to begin and load the file you had selected.)

To associate a filename extension with an application, follow these steps:

1. Select a file with the desired filename extension from a directory window.

2. Choose Associate from the File menu. You'll see a dialog box similar to the one in Figure 2-19.

FIGURE 2-19. *The Associate dialog box.*

3. Specify the application with which you want the file-name extension associated. Choose OK.

Searching Your Disk for a File

If you can't locate a file, you can use the File Manager to search for it. The File Manager will open a directory window containing a list of each matching file.

To search for a file, follow these steps:

1. Select the drive and—optionally—the directory you want to search.

2. Choose Search from the File menu. You'll see a dialog box similar to the one in Figure 2-20.

FIGURE 2-20. *The Search dialog box.*

3. Type in the name of the file you want to search for.

NOTE: *The File Manager supports wildcards (? and *) in file-names. The question mark represents any single character, and the asterisk represents any sequence of characters. For example, ?.DOC represents any one character filename that ends in DOC, whereas *.DOC represents any filename that has an extension of DOC.*

4. Select the Search Entire Disk check box if you want the File Manager to search the entire disk. Otherwise, the File Manager searches only the current directory and its subdirectories. Choose OK.

Moving Files and Directories

To move files and directories, follow these steps:

1. Open a directory window that displays the files and directories you want to move. Open the directory window to which you want to move the files and directories. Make a portion of both windows visible.

2. Select the files and directories to move.

3. Hold down the Alt key, and drag the files and directories into the new directory window.

4. If the File Manager displays a dialog box asking you to confirm the move, choose Yes.

1. Select the files and directories you want to move.

2. Choose Move from the File menu, or press F7. You'll see a dialog box similar to the one in Figure 2-21.

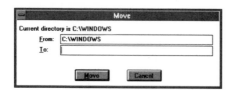

FIGURE 2-21. *The Move dialog box.*

3. Type in the pathname of the directory to which you want the files and directories moved. Choose Move.

Copying Files and Directories

To copy files and directories, follow these steps:

1. Open a directory window that displays the files and directories you want to copy. Open the directory window to which you want to copy the files and directories. Make a portion of both windows visible.

2. Select the files and directories to copy.

3. Hold down the Ctrl key, and drag the selected files and directories into the new window.

4. If the File Manager displays a dialog box asking you to confirm the copy, choose Yes.

1. Select the files and directories you want to copy.

2. Choose Copy from the File menu, or press F8. You'll see a dialog box similar to the one in Figure 2-22.

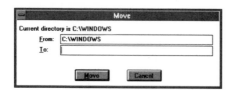

FIGURE 2-22. *The Copy dialog box.*

3. Type in the pathname of the directory to which you want the files and directories copied. Choose Copy.

Deleting a File or Directory

The File Manager lets you delete both files and directories. Note that when you delete a directory, all files and sub-directories in that directory are also deleted.

To delete a file or directory, follow these steps:

1. Select the file or directory to delete.

2. Choose Delete from the File menu, or press the Del key. You'll see a dialog box similar to the one in Figure 2-23.

FIGURE 2-23. *The Delete dialog box.*

3. Choose Delete.

4. If the File Manager displays a dialog box to confirm the deletion, choose Yes.

Renaming a File or Directory

To rename a file or directory, follow these steps:

1. Select the file or directory to rename.

2. Choose Rename from the File menu. You'll see a dialog box similar to the one in Figure 2-24.

FIGURE 2-24. *The Rename dialog box.*

3. Type in the new name. Choose Rename.

Assigning File Attributes

The File Manager lets you assign new file attributes to one or more files. The following list describes the available attributes:

File Attribute	Meaning
Read Only	Prevents the file from being changed or deleted
Archive	Identifies the file as needing to be backed up
Hidden	Prevents the file from appearing in a DOS directory list
System	Identifies a special DOS file

To assign file attributes to one or more files, follow these steps:

1. Select the desired files.

2. Choose Change Attributes from the File menu. You'll see a dialog box similar to the one in Figure 2-25.

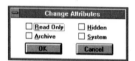

FIGURE 2-25. *The Change Attributes dialog box.*

3. Select a check box to assign the associated attribute, or deselect the check box to remove the associated attribute. Choose OK.

Using the Disk Menu

The Disk menu lets you copy, label, and format disks, as well as connect to network drives. The following list describes the items available on the Disk menu.

Menu Item	Function
Copy Diskette	Copies the contents of one floppy disk to another
Label Disk	Assigns a volume label to a disk
Format Diskette	Formats a floppy disk

Menu Item	Function
Make System Diskette	Makes a disk a boot disk
Connect Net Drive	Connects your computer to a network drive
Disconnect Net Drive	Disconnects your computer from a network drive

Copying One Floppy Disk to Another

The File Manager lets you copy the contents of one floppy disk to a second floppy disk of identical size and capacity. The disk copy operation overwrites the contents of the second disk. If the second floppy disk is not formatted, the File Manager will format it for you.

To copy one floppy disk (called the *source disk*) to another floppy disk (called the *destination disk*), follow these steps:

1. Insert the source disk into a disk drive. If you have dual disk drives of the same size and capacity, insert the destination disk into the second disk drive.

2. Select the drive the source disk is in.

3. Choose Copy Diskette from the Disk menu. You'll see the dialog box shown in Figure 2-26.

FIGURE 2-26. *The Copy Diskette dialog box.*

4. Choose the drive letter of the destination disk. (On single floppy-disk drive systems, the source and destination drives will be the same.) Choose OK.

5. A dialog box will appear, asking you to verify the copy operation. Choose Copy.

Labeling a Disk

A volume label is an 11-character name you can assign to a disk to improve your disk organization. To assign a volume label to a disk, follow these steps:

1. Select the drive containing the disk you want to label.

2. Choose Label Disk from the Disk menu. You'll see a dialog box similar to the one in Figure 2-27, possibly containing the existing volume label.

FIGURE 2-27. *The Label Disk dialog box.*

3. Type in the desired volume label, and choose OK.

Formatting a Floppy Disk

To format a floppy disk with the File Manager, follow these steps:

1. Insert the floppy disk into a drive.

2. Choose Format Diskette from the Disk menu.

3. If your computer has more than one floppy-disk drive, a dialog box will appear, asking you to select the disk to format.

4. You'll see a dialog box warning that the format operation will overwrite the existing contents of the disk. Choose Format. You'll see a dialog box similar to the one in Figure 2-28.

FIGURE 2-28. *The Format Diskette dialog box.*

5. To format a high-density disk (1.2 MB or 1.44 MB), select the High Capacity check box. To format a low-density disk, deselect the High Capacity check box. If you want to be able to boot your computer from the disk, select the Make System Disk check box.

6. Choose OK, or press Enter.

Creating a System Disk

Before you can boot your computer from a disk, the disk must contain some special files. To put these files on a disk, select the Make System Disk check box when formatting the disk.

Connecting to a Network Drive

If you've installed a network, your computer can connect to network drives. (A network drive is a drive on another computer that is also connected to the network.) To connect your computer to a network drive, follow these steps:

1. Choose Connect Net Drive from the Disk menu. You'll see a dialog box similar to the one in Figure 2-29.

FIGURE 2-29. *The Connect Network Drive dialog box.*

2. Select a drive letter for the network drive.

3. Type in the network pathname required to locate the drive, or select a previously connected pathname using the Previous button.

NOTE: *If you're not sure of the network pathname, you might be able to use the Browse button to view available pathnames.*

4. Type in the drive's password, if required.

5. If you want to record this connection in the previous connection list, select the Add to Previous List check box.

6. Choose Connect.

Disconnecting from a Network Drive

To disconnect from a network drive, follow these steps:

1. If the drive from which you want to disconnect is the current drive, select a different drive.

2. Choose Disconnect Net Drive. You'll see a dialog box similar to the one in Figure 2-30.

FIGURE 2-30. *The Disconnect Drive dialog box.*

3. Select the drive you want to disconnect.

4. The File Manager will display a dialog box asking you to confirm the disconnection. Choose OK, or press Enter.

Determining the Amount of Available Memory

To determine the amount of available memory on your system, choose About from the Help menu. You'll see a dialog box similar to Figure 2-31, displaying Windows information and the amount of available memory.

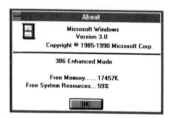

FIGURE 2-31. *The About dialog box.*

Controlling Confirmation Dialog Boxes

By default, the File Manager displays a dialog box confirming several operations, such as replacement and deletion of files. You can control whether these confirmation dialog boxes appear by using the Options menu. The following list describes the available confirmations:

Confirmation	Action
Confirm on Delete	A warning before deleting files
Confirm on Subtree Delete	A warning before deleting a subdirectory
Confirm on Replace	A warning before overwriting an existing file
Confirm on Mouse Operation	A warning before copying or moving files dragged by a mouse

To enable or disable one or more confirmations, follow these steps:

1. Choose Confirmation from the Options menu. You'll see a dialog box similar to the one in Figure 2-32.

FIGURE 2-32. *The Confirmation dialog box.*

2. Select a check box to enable confirmation on that operation. Deselect the check box to turn confirmation off. Choose OK or press Enter when you're satisfied with the confirmation settings.

Other File Manager Options

By using the Options menu, you can customize the File Manager to your liking, as described in the following list. A check mark in front of a menu item means that the menu item is active.

Menu Item	Function
Lower Case	Controls whether file and directory names are displayed in lowercase letters
Status Bar	Controls whether the status bar appears at the bottom of the File Manager window
Minimize on Use	Controls whether the File Manager is minimized when another application is run

Exiting the File Manager

To exit the File Manager, follow these steps:

1. Double-click on the File Manager's Control button, or choose Exit from the File menu. You will see a dialog box similar to the one in Figure 2-33.

FIGURE 2-33. *The Exit File Manager dialog box.*

2. Select the Save Settings check box if you want to save View or Options changes. Choose OK, or press Enter.

THE PRINT MANAGER

When you print from a Windows application, the application sends the print file to the Print Manager. The Print Manager works in the background, sending files to the printer while you continue working. As you send files to the Print Manager, it forms a print queue—a list of files waiting to be printed.

NOTE: *When you install Windows, Setup lets you identify and configure one or more printers. If you later add or change a printer, choose the Control Panel icon from the Program Manager window, and then choose the Printers icon to inform Windows of the change.*

There are actually two types of print queues: *local* and *network*. A local queue is a list of files waiting to be sent to a printer attached to your computer, whereas a network queue is a list of files waiting to be printed on a network printer.

When you send files to a local queue, the Print Manager icon appears at the bottom of your desktop. By choosing this icon, you can view, rearrange, or delete files in the local print queue, as well as set several options that control how the Print Manager behaves. (Most networks don't allow you to do these things to a network queue.)

Viewing Queued Files

To view the names of the files in the print queue, choose the Print Manager icon. The Print Manager window—similar to Figure 2-34—will appear on your screen.

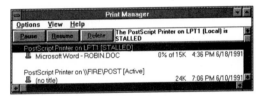

FIGURE 2-34. *The Print Manager window.*

If your computer has multiple printers or is attached to a network printer, you'll see information about each printer's queue.

Displaying Size, Time, and Date Information

By default, the Print Manager displays each file's size and the time and date you sent the file to be printed. To toggle this information on and off, choose Print File Size and Time/Date Sent from the View menu. A check mark in front of a menu item means the menu item is active.

Viewing Network Print Queues

By default, the Print Manager displays the names of only those files that you have sent to the network print queue. To view all files in a network queue, select the queue and choose Selected Net Queue from the View menu. You'll see a dialog box—similar to Figure 2-35—listing all files in the network queue.

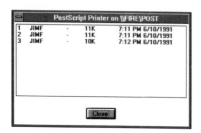

FIGURE 2-35. *A list of files in the network queue.*

Viewing Other Network Queues

In some networks, the Print Manager lets you view network print queues for other printers connected to the network. To view the print queue for a printer your computer is not connected to, follow these steps:

1. Choose Other Net Queue from the View menu.

2. When the dialog box appears, type the desired queue name and choose View.

3. Choose Close when you've finished.

Updating the Status of a Network Queue

When it is running as a window, Print Manager automatically updates the status of network queues periodically. You can also update the status manually. To manually update the status of network queues, choose Update Net Queues from the View menu.

Changing the Print Queue Order

To change the position of a file in a print queue, follow these steps:

 Drag the filename to its new position.

 Select the filename, and move it to its new position using Ctrl+Up arrow or Ctrl+Down arrow.

Removing Files from the Print Queue

To remove a file from the print queue, select its filename, and then choose Delete. The Print Manager will display a dialog box to confirm the deletion.

NOTE: *Your network might not allow you to remove files from a network queue.*

Controlling the Print Manager's Priority

The Print Manager works as a background task, printing files at the same time as you are running other applications. To do this, your computer spends some time running applications and some time printing files. Use the Options menu to set the Print Manager's *priority,* which controls how much time your computer spends printing files. The following list describes the priority possibilities:

Menu Item	Result
Low Priority	Your computer spends more time running applications than printing files. Applications run quickly, but files take a long time to print.
Medium Priority	Your computer spends an equal amount of time running applications and printing files. This is the default setting.
High Priority	Your computer spends more time printing files than running applications. Files print quickly, but applications might be sluggish.

Pausing and Resuming Printing

At times you might need to temporarily stop a local queue from printing files. (Most network software will not let you suspend or resume a network queue.) Using the Print Manager's Pause and Resume buttons, you can temporarily stop and later restart a queue printing files.

Pausing Printing

To temporarily stop a queue from printing files, follow these steps:

1. Select the queue.

2. Choose the Pause button.

Resuming Printing

To resume printing from a queue, follow these steps:

1. Select the queue.

2. Choose the Resume button.

Handling Printing Problems

Because it operates in the background, the Print Manager needs a way to let you know when something goes wrong (when the printer is out of paper, for example). The Options menu lets you specify how the Print Manager should provide such information. The following list describes the possibilities.

Menu Item	Result
Always Alert	Print Manager immediately displays a message dialog box.
Flash if Inactive	Print Manager beeps once and then flashes the Print Manager title bar or icon until you enlarge the Print Manager icon or select the Print Manager window.
Ignore if Inactive	Print Manager ignores the problem. (The printer status is changed to *stalled*.)

Closing the Print Manager

To close the Print Manager, double-click on the Control menu button or choose Exit from the Options menu. Closing the Print Manager deletes all files in all print queues, so the Print Manager will display a dialog box asking you to confirm the deletions.

THE TASK LIST

Windows lets you run several applications at the same time, each within its own window. To move among these windows quickly, you can either click in a window or use the Task List.

Activating the Task List

To activate the Task List, double-click your mouse anywhere on the desktop (outside of windows and away from icons), or press Ctrl+Esc. You'll see a dialog box similar to Figure 2-36.

FIGURE 2-36. *The Task List dialog box.*

Using the Task List

To move to an application, simply double-click on the desired application name, or use the arrow keys to select the application name and then choose Switch To.

Stopping Applications with the Task List

You can also use the Task List to stop applications. Simply select the name of the application, and choose End Task. If the application has open documents, Windows will prompt you to save the changes.

Canceling the Task List

When you've finished using the Task List, click on Cancel or press Esc.

Part III

Customizing and Optimizing Windows

Windows lets you customize several features, ensuring that your computer does the best possible job of suiting your needs and providing a comfortable working environment. In this section, you'll learn to take advantage of Windows' versatility.

THE CONTROL PANEL

At the heart of Windows customization is the *Control Panel*. The Control Panel provides you with a variety of applications that let you set up Windows in the way that works best for you.

To use the Control Panel, expand the Control Panel icon from the Program Manager window. You'll see the window shown in Figure 3-1.

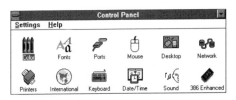

FIGURE 3-1. *The Control Panel and its applications.*

Control Panel applications appear as icons within the Control Panel window. These applications perform the following tasks:

Change screen colors (*Color*)

Configure serial ports (*Ports*)

Customize your desktop (*Desktop*)

Specify international settings (*International*)

Set the date and time (*Date/Time*)

Set network options (*Network*)

Manage fonts (*Fonts*)

Customize mouse (*Mouse*)

Configure printers (*Printers*)

Set the keyboard repeat rate (*Keyboard*)

Disable warning beeps (*Sound*)

Specify which applications have priority (*386 Enhanced*)

The following sections describe how to use each of these applications.

Changing Screen Colors

The Color application lets you change the colors used for different areas of the screen, such as the desktop, window background, window borders, window title bar, and so on. When you run the Color application, you'll see a dialog box similar to the one shown in Figure 3-2.

FIGURE 3-2. *The Color dialog box.*

This dialog box represents the different areas of your desktop—windows, window borders, title bars, and so on.

Using a Predefined Color Scheme

Windows comes with several predefined color combinations. To use a predefined color combination, follow these steps:

1. Open the Color Schemes drop-down list.

2. Select a color scheme from the list. The colors in the dialog box change to reflect your selection.

3. When you see a color scheme you like, choose OK. Windows adopts the new color scheme.

Changing the Color of a Desktop Element

To change the color of a particular screen element, such as window title bars or scroll bars, follow these steps:

1. Choose Color Palette >>. You'll see a dialog box similar to the one shown in Figure 3-3.

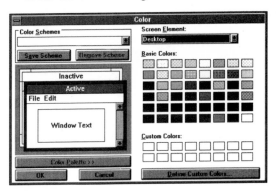

FIGURE 3-3. *The Color dialog box with palette.*

2. Open the Screen Element drop-down list, and select the screen element whose color you want to change.

3. Select the new color, and choose OK.

Creating a Color

The Color application also lets you create your own colors. To do so, follow these steps:

1. Move to the Custom Colors field, and select a box for the new color.

2. Choose Define Custom Colors. You'll see a dialog box similar to the one shown in Figure 3-4.

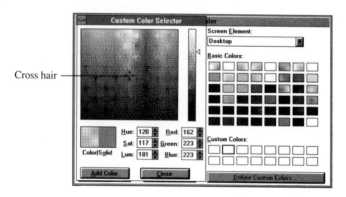

Cross hair

FIGURE 3-4. *The Custom Color Selector dialog box.*

3. Select the color you want by following these steps:

Click within the Custom Color Selector to move the cross hair to the desired color scheme. Then adjust the brightness of the color by scrolling in the vertical bar to the right of the Custom Color Selector. The Color/Solid box reflects your current selection.

Move to the boxes beneath the Custom Color Selector, and specify a value for each. Valid values are as follows: Hue 0 through 239; Sat(uration) and Lum(inosity) 0 through 240; Red, Green, and Blue 0 through 255. The Color/Solid box reflects your current selection.

The following diagram shows how these numbers are interpreted in the Custom Color Selector:

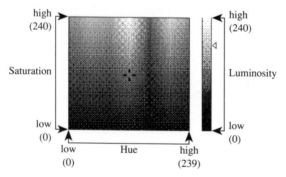

4. Choose Add Color.

5. Choose Close.

Managing Fonts

A *font* is a complete set of characters of a certain size. A *font file* is a file that contains a font. To add a font, you load a font file into your computer. When you choose the Fonts icon in the Control Panel window, you'll see a dialog box similar to the one shown in Figure 3-5.

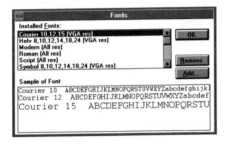

FIGURE 3-5. *The Fonts dialog box.*

Adding a Font

To add a font, follow these steps:

1. Choose Add. You'll see a dialog box similar to the one shown in Figure 3-6.

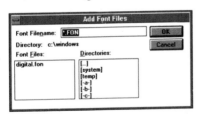

FIGURE 3-6. *The Add Font Files dialog box.*

2. Put the disk containing the font file in a floppy-disk drive.

3. From the Directories box, choose the drive that contains the font file. The Font Files box displays all font files on the specified drive.

4. Select the font file from the Font Files box, and choose OK.

Removing a Font

To remove a font, follow these steps:

1. Choose Fonts from the Control Panel window.

2. From the Installed Fonts box, select the font you want to remove.

3. Choose Remove.

4. You'll see a second dialog box asking you to confirm the font removal. Choose Yes to remove the font, or choose No to cancel the procedure.

Configuring Serial Ports

Serial ports let you connect a mouse, modem, or other hardware device to your computer. As part of the connection process, you must set the communication parameters of each serial port to match the parameters of the device. (The manual for your hardware device describes its parameters.) To do so, expand the Ports icon from the Control Panel window. You'll see the dialog box shown in Figure 3-7.

Communications Terminology

If you're going to set up ports, you'll need to be familiar with the following terms in the Ports dialog box:

baud rate—The speed with which information is transferred through the port

data bits—The number of bits contained in each packet of information

parity—The method of error-checking that both devices agree to use

stop bits—The amount of time between transmitted characters

flow control—The type of handshaking method used

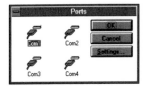

FIGURE 3-7. *The Ports dialog box.*

Setting Communication Parameters

To set a port's communication parameters, follow these steps:

1. Select the desired port.

2. Choose Settings. You'll see a dialog box similar to the one shown in Figure 3-8.

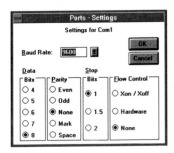

FIGURE 3-8. *The Ports-Settings dialog box.*

3. Select Baud Rate. Open the drop-down list, and select the rate desired.

4. Select an option button in the Data Bits box.

5. Select an option button in the Parity box.

6. Select an option button in the Stop Bits box.

7. Select an option button in the Flow Control box.

8. When you've finished setting the port's communication parameters, choose OK.

Customizing the Mouse

If you have a mouse, you can use the Control Panel's Mouse icon to control how fast the mouse pointer moves and how fast you must double-click to choose items. You can even use the Mouse icon to swap the actions of the left and right mouse buttons (a handy option for left-handed Mouse users).

To customize your mouse, expand the Mouse icon from the Control Panel window. You'll see a dialog box similar to the one shown in Figure 3-9.

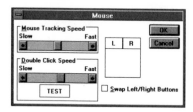

FIGURE 3-9. *The Mouse dialog box.*

Setting Mouse Tracking Speed

To set mouse tracking speed (the speed at which the mouse cursor moves across the screen), simply drag the scroll box to the desired area in the scroll bar.

Setting Double-Click Speed

To set the double-click speed, simply drag the scroll box to the desired area in the scroll bar. To test the double-click speed, double-click on the box labeled *TEST*. If the box changes color, your double-click was fast enough to choose an item.

Swapping Left/Right Buttons

To swap the function of the left and right mouse buttons (helpful if you're a lefty), click on the Swap Left/Right Buttons.

Choose OK when you've finished customizing your mouse.

Customizing Your Desktop

The default Windows desktop, while fully functional, is rather boring. You can, however, change the look of the desktop, the width of window borders, the cursor blink rate,

and other items. To do so, expand the Desktop icon from
the Control Panel. You'll see a dialog box similar to the
one shown in Figure 3-10.

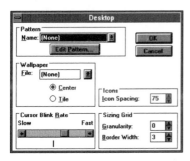

FIGURE 3-10. *The Desktop dialog box.*

Selecting a Background Pattern

By default, your desktop is a solid color. You can change
the desktop to a predefined background pattern, create your
own background pattern, or even use a graphics file created
by Paintbrush or a similar application.

Windows provides several predefined background patterns,
as shown in Figure 3-11.

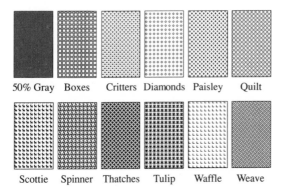

FIGURE 3-11. *Predefined background patterns.*

To use a predefined background pattern, follow these steps:

1. Open the Pattern Name drop-down list.

2. Choose a background pattern.

Creating Your Own Pattern

NOTE: *You need a mouse to create a new background pattern. You cannot create a new background pattern from the keyboard.*

If none of the predefined background patterns suit your tastes, you can create your own. To do so, follow these steps:

1. Choose Edit Pattern from the Pattern field. You'll see a dialog box similar to the one shown in Figure 3-12.

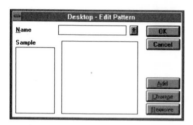

FIGURE 3-12. *The Desktop-Edit Pattern dialog box.*

2. Type in a name for your pattern, but do *not* press Enter.

3. Click inside the large center box. A large black square appears. Click on the square, and it disappears. The sample box shows what the pattern will look like on the desktop.

   □ To paint, click on a blank area and drag.

   □ To erase, click on a filled area and drag.

4. When you've finished editing, choose Add.

Editing an Existing Pattern

NOTE: *You need a mouse to edit a background pattern. You cannot edit a background pattern from the keyboard.*

To save time, you can also edit an existing background pattern. To do so, follow these steps:

1. Open the Pattern Name drop-down list.

2. Select the pattern to edit.

3. Choose Edit Pattern.

4. Click inside the large center box. A large black square appears. Click on the square, and it disappears. The sample box shows what the pattern will look like on the desktop.

5. When you've finished editing, choose Change.

6. Choose OK.

Deleting a Pattern

To delete a pattern, follow these steps:

1. Open the Pattern Name drop-down list.

2. Select the pattern to remove.

3. Choose Edit Pattern.

4. Choose Remove.

5. A dialog box asks you to confirm the deletion. Choose Yes to remove the pattern, or choose No to cancel the procedure.

6. Choose OK.

Selecting Wallpaper

When it comes to customizing your desktop, you're not limited to background patterns. You can also use *wallpaper* (a graphics image) to add an interesting flair. Windows provides several predefined wallpapers, one of which is the crinkled paper shown in Figure 3-13.

FIGURE 3-13. *One of several wallpapers available for use.*

To select a wallpaper, follow these steps:

1. Open the Wallpaper drop-down list.

2. Select the desired wallpaper.

3. Select either Center or Tile. Center centers the wallpaper on your desktop. Tile repeats the wallpaper as many times as necessary to completely cover your desktop.

NOTE: *The wallpaper will not appear until you close the Desktop dialog box.*

4. Choose OK.

Changing the Cursor Blink Rate

To increase or decrease the rate at which your cursor blinks, follow these steps:

Click on the left or right arrow in the Cursor Blink Rate scroll bar to make the cursor blink rate a little slower or faster, or drag the scroll box to rapidly change the rate.

1. Select the Cursor Blink Rate Scroll Bar.

2. Use the arrow keys to move the Cursor Blink Rate scroll box. Watch the scroll box to determine the desired rate.

3. Choose OK.

Changing the Icon Spacing

Icon spacing is the distance (in pixels) Windows places between icons. By increasing this distance, you can prevent a long icon name from obscuring another icon name. To change the icon spacing, follow these steps:

Click on the up or down arrow in the Icon Spacing box to increase or decrease the value for icon spacing.

1. Select the Icon Spacing text box, and type in a new value for icon spacing.

2. Choose OK.

Using the Sizing Grid Box

The Sizing Grid box contains two fields. The first, *Granularity,* is not a box you need to concern yourself with.

The second, *Border Width,* lets you set the size of the window borders (which, by default, are 3 pixels wide).

To change the window border width, follow these steps:

 Click on the up or down arrows in the Border Width box to increase or decrease the border width.

 Select the Border Width text box, and type in a value for the new border width.

Configuring a Printer

If you add or change a printer, you must use the Printers application to inform Windows of the change. When you expand the Printers icon from the Control Panel, you'll see a dialog box similar to the one shown in Figure 3-14.

FIGURE 3-14. *The Printers dialog box.*

Adding a Printer

To add a printer, follow these steps:

1. Choose Add Printer >>. The dialog box will change to look similar to Figure 3-15.

2. Select the desired printer from the List of Printers list box.

3. Choose Install.

4. A dialog box similar to the one shown in Figure 3-16 will appear. Insert the requested disk into the disk drive, and choose OK.

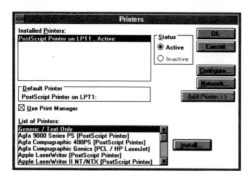

FIGURE 3-15. *The Printers dialog box, with a list of available printers.*

FIGURE 3-16. *The Control Panel-Printers dialog box.*

Setting Up a Printer

To configure a printer, follow these steps:

1. Select the printer you want to configure from the Installed Printers list box.

2. Choose Configure. You'll see a dialog box similar to the one shown in Figure 3-17.

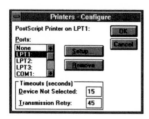

FIGURE 3-17. *The Printers-Configure dialog box.*

3. Select a port for the printer, and then choose OK.

NOTE: *If you need to set specific printer options for the printer you're configuring, choose Setup in the Printers-Configure dialog box. You'll see a dialog box with options specific to the selected printer. See your printer's manual for the proper settings for these options.*

Removing a Printer

To remove a printer, follow these steps:

1. Select the name of the printer to be removed from the Installed Printers list.

2. Choose Configure.

3. Choose Remove. You'll see a dialog box asking you to confirm the printer removal. Choose Yes to remove the printer, or No to cancel the procedure.

Selecting the Default Printer

If your computer has multiple printers attached, you must select one printer as the default printer. Unless you specify otherwise, all print files are sent to the default printer. You can change the default printer at any time. To select a default printer, follow these steps:

1. Select a printer from the Installed Printers list.

2. Select the Active option button in the Status box.

NOTE: *A printer must be configured before it can become active.*

Specifying International Settings

To specify the date, time, number, and currency formats—as well as the keyboard layout—that Windows should use, expand the Control Panel's International icon. You'll see a dialog box similar to the one shown in Figure 3-18.

The following paragraphs describe the fields in this dialog box. To change the value of one of the first four fields, follow these steps:

1. Select the field, and open its drop-down list box.

2. Choose an item from the list.

FIGURE 3-18. *The International dialog box.*

Country This field controls the country whose date, time, number, and currency formats Windows uses. When you choose a country, Windows changes the formats in the Date, Time, Currency, and Number boxes (at the bottom of the dialog box) to reflect the default formats used in the country.

Language This field controls the language Windows applications use when sorting lists and converting the case of letters.

Keyboard Layout This field controls the keyboard layout Windows uses.

Measurement This field controls the measurement system Windows uses.

List Separator This field controls the symbol used to separate items in a list. To use a different symbol, select the List Separator box and type in the new symbol.

NOTE: *Each Country has a default symbol set. You'll see the "correct" symbol set. To override any default setting associated with a country, simply use the dialog box as described above.*

Date Format You can change the format used to display the date within applications that have a date function. For example, you can vary the order of month-day-year or change the punctuation used to separate the parts of the date. To change the date format, choose Change in the Date Format box. You'll see a dialog box similar to the one shown in Figure 3-19.

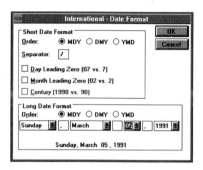

FIGURE 3-19. *The International-Date Format dialog box.*

The Short Date Format displays the date as three numbers representing the month, day, and year. You specify the order and number of digits for each part of the date. The Long Date Format displays the date as a combination of words and numbers. Select the options that suit your needs.

Time Format You can choose either the 12-hour or 24-hour format, specifying the separator between the parts and displaying numbers representing the hours before 10 with a leading zero if you want. To change the time format, choose Change in the Time Format box. You'll see a dialog box similar to the one shown in Figure 3-20. Select the options that suit your needs.

FIGURE 3-20. *The International-Time Format dialog box.*

Currency Format To change the currency format, choose Change in the Currency Format box. You'll see a dialog box similar to the one shown in Figure 3-21. Select the options that suit your needs.

FIGURE 3-21. *The International-Currency Format dialog box.*

Number Format You can control the way numbers are displayed in Windows and in many Windows applications. To do so, choose Change in the Number Format box. You'll see a dialog box similar to the one shown in Figure 3-22. Select the options that suit your needs.

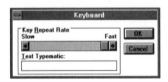

FIGURE 3-22. *The International-Number Format dialog box.*

Setting the Key Repeat Rate

The *key repeat rate* dictates how quickly a held-down key repeats. To change the key repeat rate, expand the Keyboard icon from the Control Panel. You'll see a dialog box similar to the one shown in Figure 3-23.

FIGURE 3-23. *The Keyboard dialog box.*

To change the key repeat rate, follow these steps:

Click on the left or right arrows in the Key Repeat Rate scroll bar to make the key repeat rate a little slower or faster, or drag the scroll box to rapidly change the key repeat rate.

Use the right and left arrow keys to adjust the
key repeat rate.

To test the key repeat rate, select the Typematic text box
and hold down a key. When you're satisfied with the Key
Repeat Rate, choose OK.

Setting the Computer's Date and Time

To change the computer's internal date and time, expand
the Control Panel's Date/Time icon. You'll see a dialog box
similar to the one shown in Figure 3-24.

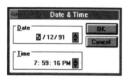

FIGURE 3-24. *The Date & Time dialog box.*

Setting the Computer's Date

To set your computer's date, follow these steps:

 1. Click on the date field you want to change.

2. Click on the Date box's up or down arrows to
   increase or decrease the value in that field.

 Use the Tab key to select the date field you want
to change, and type in the new value for that
field.

Setting the Computer's Time

To set your computer's time, follow these steps:

 1. Click on the time field you want to change.

2. Click on the Time box's up or down arrows to
   increase or decrease the value in that field.

 Use the Tab key to select the time field you want
to change, and type in the new value for that
field.

When you've finished setting the date and time,
choose OK.

Disabling Warning Beeps

By default, Windows beeps when you try to do something
you are not allowed to do. (For example, you'll hear a beep
if you try to ignore an active dialog box.) You can *disable*
(turn off) the beep from the Control Panel by following
these steps:

1. Expand the Sound icon. You'll see a dialog box similar
   to the one shown in Figure 3-25.

FIGURE 3-25. *The Sound dialog box.*

2. Deselect the Warning Beep check box, removing the X.
   Choose OK.

Setting Network Options

If your computer is connected to a network, the Control
Panel window includes a *Network* icon. If you expand this
icon, you'll see a dialog box specific to your network,
which might let you log onto the network, modify your user
name and password, and send messages to other network
users. See your network administrator for specific details.

Using 386 Enhanced Mode Options

If you own a computer that uses an 80386SX, 80386, i486SX,
i486, or compatible microprocessor, Windows runs in 386
enhanced mode. 386 enhanced mode lets one or more DOS
applications run at the same time as Windows applications.

When Windows applications and DOS applications are
running simultaneously, they sometimes will try to use
a device, such as a printer or modem, at the same time.

(Such jockeying for resources is called *device contention*.)
To specify how Windows should handle this situation, follow these steps:

1. Expand the 386 enhanced mode icon from the Control
   Panel. You'll see a dialog box similar to the one shown
   in Figure 3-26.

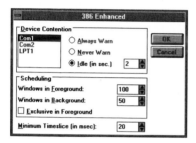

FIGURE 3-26. *The 386 Enhanced dialog box.*

2. Select the device from the Device Contention list.

3. Select the option button that best suits your needs. The
   following table describes the possibilities:

Windows Action	**Result**
Always Warn	Windows displays a warning dialog box each time an application tries to use a device already in use. The dialog box asks you which application should gain control of the device.
Never Warn	Windows lets any application use the device at any time: You receive no warning. This could result in two applications trying to use the device at the same time, with undesirable results.
Idle	Specifies the number of seconds (from 1 to 999) a device must be idle before a second application can use it freely. If a second application tries to use the device before the idle period is complete, a warning message will appear.

386 Enhanced Mode Scheduling Options

When multiple applications are running simultaneously,
Windows runs one application for awhile, switches to the

next application and runs it for a certain amount of time, repeating the process for each application. You can dictate how much time Windows spends on the application in the active window (called the *foreground* window) and how much time it spends on an application in an inactive window (called a *background* window). To do so, follow these steps:

1. Expand the 386 enhanced mode icon from the Control Panel. You'll see a dialog box similar to the one shown in Figure 3-26.

2. Select the Windows in Foreground text box, and enter a number from 1 through 10,000. The higher the number, the more time Windows spends running the foreground application.

3. Select the Windows in Background text box, and enter a number from 1 through 10,000. The higher the number, the more time Windows spends running background applications.

4. Select the Minimum Timeslice text box, and enter a number from 1 through 1000. This is the number of milliseconds (thousandths of a second) that Windows spends executing a DOS application.

5. When you've finished setting scheduling options, choose OK.

PUTTING MEMORY TO WORK

NOTE: *Memory is too complex a subject to fully cover here. For a lively and useful guide to taking full advantage of your computer's memory, see Dan Gookin's* The Microsoft Guide to Managing Memory with DOS 5 *(Microsoft Press, 1991).*

Your computer can contain as many as three types of memory: *conventional memory, extended memory,* and *expanded memory.* All IBM-PC–compatible computers have conventional memory, which is memory up to 640 KB (although some computers have less than 640 KB of conventional memory).

If your computer uses an 80286, 80386, 80386SX, i486SX, or i486 microprocessor, it probably contains extended memory. Extended memory is memory above the 1-MB mark. Computers that use the 8088 or 8086 microprocessors cannot have extended memory. As a general rule, the more extended memory you add to your computer, the faster Windows will run your applications.

Expanded memory is essentially a pool of extra memory. Using a special memory board and software, expanded memory can be mapped into a 64-KB region of *upper memory* (the 384-KB memory area between 640 KB and 1 MB). Different areas of expanded memory can be mapped into this 64-KB region. All IBM-compatible computers can use expanded memory.

If you are using an 80286-based, 80386SX-based, 80386-based, i486-based, or i486SX-based computer that has extended memory, you should be sure that your CONFIG.SYS loads HIMEM.SYS. HIMEM.SYS is an extended memory manager (provided with Windows and DOS 5) that lets your computer use extended memory. You should see a line similar to the following in your CONFIG.SYS file:

```
device=c:\dos\himem.sys
```

If you are using an 80386SX-based, 80386-based, i486-based, or i486SX-based computer and you use an application that needs expanded memory, be sure that your CONFIG.SYS file loads EMM386.EXE. EMM386.EXE uses extended memory to simulate expanded memory. You should see a line similar to the following in your CONFIG.SYS file:

```
device=c:\dos\emm386.exe
```

NOTE: *Both Windows and DOS 5 include an EMM386 device driver. The DOS 5 EMM386 device driver is called EMM386.EXE, and the Windows EMM386 device driver is called EMM386.SYS. The examples shown here use EMM386.EXE. If you don't use DOS 5, substitute EMM386.SYS for EMM386.EXE in these examples. If you own both Windows and DOS 5, use EMM386.EXE.*

Creating a RAM Disk

Many Windows applications create temporary files. You can improve Windows performance by creating a RAM disk and storing temporary files there.

To create a RAM disk, add the following line to your CONFIG.SYS file:

```
DEVICE=C:\DOS\RAMDRIVE.SYS [DiskSize
    [SectorSize [DirectoryEntries]]] [/A ¦ /E]
```

Items shown in square brackets are optional. Items separated by the pipe (¦) character are mutually exclusive— that is, you can choose only one or the other.

- *DiskSize* specifies the RAM disk's size in kilobytes, from 16 (16 KB) through 4096 (4096 KB). The default value is 64 (64 KB).

- *SectorSize* specifies the size of the RAM disk's sectors. A large sector size is good for large files, and a small sector size is good for small files. Valid numbers for *Sector-Size* are 128, 256, 512, or 1024. The default value is 512 (512 KB). If you specify *SectorSize*, you must also specify *DiskSize*.

- *DirectoryEntries* specifies the maximum number of files the RAM disk's root directory can hold, from 2 through 1024. The default is 64 (64 entries). If you provide a value for *DirectoryEntries*, you must also specify *Sector-Size* and *DiskSize*.

- The /A switch creates the RAM disk in expanded memory, whereas the /E switch creates the RAM disk in extended memory. If you do not specify /A or /E, the RAM disk is created in conventional memory.

Creating a Disk Cache

A *disk cache* is a large buffer in memory that holds information that has been written on disk. If an application needs to read that information, it reads it from the disk cache instead of the disk, thereby improving performance.

To create a disk cache, add the following line to your CON-FIG.SYS file:

```
DEVICE=C:\DOS\SMARTDRV.SYS [InitialCache]
    [MinimumCache] /A ¦ /E
```

Items shown in square brackets are optional. Items separated by the pipe (¦) character are mutually exclusive—that is, you can select only one of them.

■ *InitialCache* specifies the disk cache's starting size in kilobytes, from 128 (128 KB) through 8192 (8192 KB). As a rule, set the initial disk-cache size as large as possible. Windows will reduce the disk cache's size if necessary. The default value is 256 (256 KB).

■ *MinimumCache* specifies the smallest size in kilobytes to which Windows can reduce the disk cache. The default value is 256 (256 KB).

■ The /A switch creates the disk cache in expanded memory, whereas the /E switch creates the disk cache in extended memory. The disk cache must be created in either extended or expanded memory.

Understanding Windows Swap Files

When Windows gets low on memory, it temporarily copies information to a file on your hard disk. When the information is needed again, Windows copies it back from the file into memory. This process of moving information from memory to a file on the hard disk and back to memory again is called *swapping*. The file copied to is called a *swap file*.

By default, Windows uses a *temporary* swap file. A *permanent* swap file is often a better choice because Windows can access a permanent swap file more quickly. A permanent swap file does, however, take up hard-disk space—even when Windows is not in use. If you use Windows extensively in 386 enhanced mode, the permanent swap file will provide best performance. If you don't use Windows extensively, you might want to sacrifice performance for available hard-disk space and stick with the temporary swap file.

To create a permanent swap file, follow these steps:

1. Exit Windows, if necessary, and type the following command at the DOS prompt:

   ```
   C:\>WIN /R SWAPFILE <Enter>
   ```

   You'll see a dialog box similar to the one shown in Figure 3-27, recommending a swap-file size.

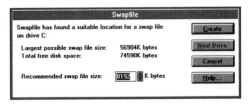

FIGURE 3-27. *The Swapfile dialog box.*

2. If you want to increase or decrease the recommended size, type in a new size, or click on the up and down arrows.

3. Choose Create to create the swap file. You'll see another dialog box telling you that the swap file has been created. Choose OK.

4. Exit, and then restart Windows.

If you later decide to change or delete the permanent swap file, repeat this procedure.

CHANGING SYSTEM SETTINGS USING SETUP

If you change your video card, mouse, keyboard, or network, you must tell Windows about the change. To do this, expand the Program Manager's Setup icon. You'll see a dialog box, similar to the one shown in Figure 3-28, that lists your existing system settings.

The Setup application lets you perform two different tasks: changing system settings and setting up applications.

Windows Setup	
<u>O</u>ptions <u>H</u>elp	
Display:	VGA
Keyboard:	Enhanced 101 or 102 key US and Non US
Mouse:	Microsoft, or IBM PS/2
Network:	Microsoft Network (or 100% compatible)
Swap file:	Permanent (16372 K bytes on Drive C:)

FIGURE 3-28. *The Windows Setup dialog box.*

Changing System Settings

To change your system settings, choose Change System Settings from the Options menu. You'll see a dialog box similar to the one shown in Figure 3-29.

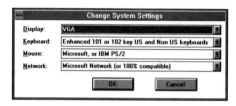

FIGURE 3-29. *The Change System Settings dialog box.*

This dialog box has drop-down lists for your Display, Keyboard, Mouse, and Network. To change a setting, follow these steps:

1. Select the setting, and open its drop-down list.

2. Choose the new setting.

3. When you've finished changing settings, choose OK. You'll see a dialog box that prompts you to restart Windows or return to DOS. To do so, choose the appropriate icon.

Adding Non-Windows Applications

If you have one or more non-Windows applications, you can let Setup search your hard disk for these applications and create an icon for each. To do this, choose Set Up Applications from the Options menu. You'll see a dialog box similar to the one shown in Figure 3-30.

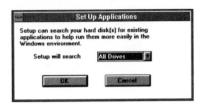

FIGURE 3-30. *The Set Up Applications dialog box.*

By default, Set Up Applications searches all nonfloppy drives in your computer. To limit the search to a specific drive, open the drop-down list and select the desired drive. Choose OK to begin the search. As Setup searches, you'll see a dialog box similar to the one shown in Figure 3-31.

FIGURE 3-31. *The Windows Setup dialog box.*

When Setup has completed the search, you'll see a dialog box similar to the one shown in Figure 3-32.

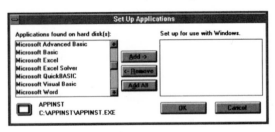

FIGURE 3-32. *The expanded Set Up Applications dialog box.*

The dialog box displays all the applications found in the search. To add all the applications, choose Add All. To add specific applications, follow these steps:

1. Select the application from the *Applications found on hard disk(s):* list box.

2. Choose Add.

If you change your mind about adding an application, follow these steps:

1. Select the application from the *Set up for use with Windows* list box.

2. Choose Remove.

3. When you've finished selecting applications, choose OK.

Setup really doesn't prepare a non-Windows application for running under Windows. Instead, it adds an icon for the application to the non-Windows Application group. For more information on running non-Windows applications, refer to the description of the PIF Editor in Part IV.

PART IV

Desktop Applications

Windows provides a powerful collection of *desktop applications,* which are designed to help you perform a variety of tasks right from the Windows desktop:

Calculator	Performs business and statistical calculations
Calendar	Manages your appointments
Cardfile	Lists information
Clock	Keeps track of the time
Notepad	Allows you to edit text
Paintbrush	Allows you to create figures and drawings
Recorder	Records Macros
Terminal	Permits telecommunications
Write	Allows you to perform word processing

To access these programs, move to the Program Manager window, and expand the Accessories window by choosing the Accessories icon. Windows displays the Accessories group window (Figure 4-1).

FIGURE 4-1. *The Accessories group window.*

This section provides an overview of each desktop accessory program, as well as an introduction to the PIF editor, which lets you describe non-Windows applications to the Windows program.

CALCULATOR

The calculator application acts as a *standard calculator* (for addition, subtraction, multiplication, and division) and as a *scientific calculator* (for trigonometric functions and statistical operations). The first time you use Calculator, you'll see the standard calculator, as shown in Figure 4-2.

FIGURE 4-2. *The standard calculator.*

Switching Calculators

To switch between the standard and scientific calculators, choose either Standard or Scientific from the View menu.

Entering Values

To enter values, click on the number buttons or enter numbers with your keyboard.

NOTE: *If you're using the keyboard, you can use the numbers from the top row of the keyboard or the numbers from the numeric keypad. If you choose to use the keypad, remember to activate the NumLock key.*

Using the Standard Calculator

To add, subtract, multiply, or divide two numbers, follow these steps:

1. Enter the first number's digits.

2. Click on the symbol of the desired operation, or press the corresponding keyboard key.

3. Enter the second number's digits.

4. Click on the equal sign, or press your keyboard's equal-sign key.

The following table lists calculator buttons, the keyboard equivalent of each button, and the purpose of each standard calculator function:

Button	Keyboard Key	Function
C	Esc	Clears the current calculation
CE	Del	Clears the current value
Back	Backspace/ Left arrow	Clears the rightmost digit of the current value
MC	Ctrl+C	Clears the contents of memory
MR	Ctrl+R	Recalls the value stored in memory
M+	Ctrl+P	Adds the current value to the value in memory and places the result in memory
MS	Ctrl+M	Stores the current value in memory
+/–	F9	Changes the current value's sign
1/X	R	Calculates the reciprocal of the current value
sqrt	@	Calculates the square root of the current value
%	%	Treats the current value as a percentage

Using the Scientific Calculator

The scientific calculator appears as shown in Figure 4-3.

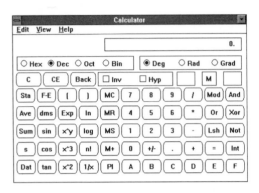

FIGURE 4-3. *The scientific calculator.*

With the scientific calculator you can work with hexadecimal, decimal, octal, or binary numbers and specify an angle's units of measure in degrees, radians, or gradients.

The following table lists the button, keyboard equivalent, and purpose of each scientific calculator function:

Button	Keyboard Key	Function
Sta	Ctrl+S	Activates the calculator's statistics box and buttons
Ave	Ctrl+A	Averages statistics-box values
Sum	Ctrl+T	Adds statistics-box values
s	Ctrl+D	Calculates the standard deviation of statistics-box values
Dat	Ins	Places the current value into a statistics box
F-E	v	Toggles scientific notation on and off (can only be used with decimal numbers)
dms	m	Converts the current value from degrees to degrees, minutes, and seconds
sin	s	Calculates the sine of the current value
cos	o	Calculates the cosine of the current value
tan	t	Calculates the tangent of the current value

Button	Keyboard Key	Function
Exp	x	Enables entry of numbers in scientific notation
x^y	y	Raises the current value to the power of the value you type next
x^3	#	Calculates the cubes of the current value
x^2	@	Calculates the squares of the current value
ln	n	Calculates the natural logarithm of the current value
log	l	Calculates the base-10 logarithm of the current value
n!	!	Calculates the factorial of the current value
Mod	%	Calculates the remainder of the current value divided by the value you type next
Or	¦	Calculates the bitwise OR of the current value and the value you type next
Lsh	<	Calculates current value left-shifted by the number of bit positions you type next
And	&	Calculates bitwise AND of the current value and the value you type next
Xor	^	Calculates the bitwise exclusive OR of the current value and the value you type next
Not	~	Calculates the bitwise inverse of the current value
Int	;	Calculates the integer portion of a decimal number
PI	P	Makes Pi the current value
ABCDEF	ABCDEF	Enters the hexadecimal digits A through F
Inv	I	Selects the inverse function for sin, cos, tan, Pi (results in 2 Pi), ln, log, Ave, Sum, s, x^y, x^3, x^2

Button	Keyboard Key	Function
Deg	F2	Selects degrees as an angle's unit of measure
Rad	F3	Selects radians as an angle's unit of measure
Grad	F4	Selects gradients as an angle's unit of measure
Hex	F5	Selects hexadecimal base
Dec	F6	Selects decimal base
Oct	F7	Selects octal base
Bin	F8	Selects binary base
Dword *	F2	Displays current value's 32-bit representation
Word *	F3	Displays current value's lower 16-bit representation
Byte *	F4	Displays current value's lower 8-bit representation

* Indicates a button available only in a nondecimal base.

Performing Statistical Calculations

To perform statistical calculations, choose the scientific calculator's Sta button. Calculator opens a window called the *statistics box* which, like any window, can be moved to a convenient location on your screen. The statistics box appears as shown in Figure 4-4.

FIGURE 4-4. *The Statistics Box dialog box.*

To enter numbers into the statistics box, follow these steps:

1. Activate the Calculator window by clicking on the calculator or by typing *R*.

2. Enter the desired value.

3. Press the calculator's Dat button.

You can enter as many values as you want. After entering all values, you can use the calculator's statistical functions. If you enter more than six values into the statistics box, a vertical scroll bar appears at the right side of the box. You can use this scroll bar to scroll through the values. The following table describes each statistics-box button, as well as its keyboard equivalent, and purpose:

Button	Keyboard Key	Function
Ret	R	Returns to the Calculator window from the statistics box
Load	L	Copies the value selected in the statistics box to Calculator
CD	C	Deletes current value of statistics box
CAD	A	Deletes all values from statistics box

CALENDAR

Calendar is an electronic daily and monthly planner. Using Calendar, you can enter and track your appointments for today, next week, or even several months from now. Depending on your preference, Calendar lets you combine or separate your schedules. In other words, you can keep one large master schedule of all your appointments, or you can create individual schedules for home, work, and leisure activities. If your computer connects to a local area network, you can even exchange calendars with other users to resolve scheduling conflicts. Using Calendar's built-in alarm capabilities, you can be reminded of key appointments. Calendar lets you work with a daily or monthly planner, as shown in Figures 4-5 and 4-6.

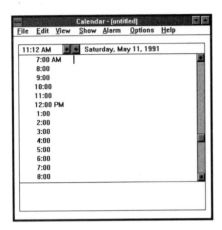

FIGURE 4-5. *The daily planner.*

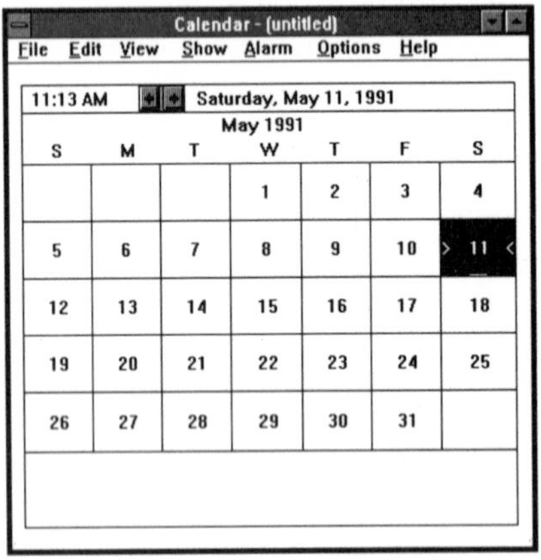

FIGURE 4-6. *The monthly planner.*

Calendar File Operations

Calendar stores your schedules on disk in files with the CAL extension. Calendar's File menu lets you save a new schedule, save the existing schedule, print appointments, or open a different calendar file, such as VACATION.CAL. The following table briefly describes Calendar's File menu:

Option	Function
New	Creates a new calendar, first prompting you to save or discard changes to the current calendar
Open	Displays a dialog box that lets you load an existing calendar file
Save	Saves schedule changes to an existing calendar file
Save As	Lets you save a schedule under a new name
Print	Prints appointments for the range of days you specify
Exit	Closes the Calendar window

The first time you start Calendar, you'll see the daily planner.

Choosing Your Planner

To select the planner you want to use, simply choose Day or Month from the View menu, or press F8 (daily planner) or F9 (monthly planner).

Calendar's Daily Planner

Calendar's daily planner lets you enter appointments for a 24-hour day.

Using the Daily Planner

To move inside the daily planner, use the arrow keys, or drag the vertical scroll bar using your mouse. To schedule an appointment, simply type the appointment at the correct time.

Changing Calendar's Timing

By default, Calendar displays appointments at 1-hour intervals. If you need finer scheduling resolution, Calendar lets you use 15-minute and 30-minute intervals.

To change the daily appointment calendar's time interval, choose Day Settings from the Options menu. You'll see a dialog box similar to Figure 4-7.

FIGURE 4-7. *The Day Settings dialog box.*

Interval lets you select 15-minute, 30-minute, or 60-minute intervals. *Hour Format* lets you specify a 12-hour clock with A.M./P.M. format or a 24-hour military clock. *Starting Time* lets you specify the time you want to appear at the top of the daily calendar when you first view it. Select the options you desire, and then choose OK.

Viewing Other Appointments

Calendar lets you view a previous or future day's appointments. To do so, click on the arrows in the line that displays the date and time, or press Ctrl+PgUp to view the previous day and Ctrl+PgDn to view the following day. To view the schedule for a day more than a few days prior to—or following—the current day, choose Date from Calendar's Show menu. A dialog box asks for the date. Type in the date you want to view, and then choose OK.

Setting Alarms for Appointments

In the daily planner you can set alarms that notify you of appointments. To set an alarm, follow these steps:

1. Select the day for which you want the alarm set.

2. Click on the desired time, or move the cursor to the desired time by using the arrow keys.

3. Set the alarm by choosing Set from Calendar's Alarm menu.

A bell symbol—indicating that the alarm is set—appears to the left of the time.

Early Warning

By default, Calendar activates the alarm at the specified time. To sound the alarm a few minutes prior to the

specified time, choose Controls from the Alarm menu.
You'll see a dialog box similar to the one shown in Figure
4-8.

FIGURE 4-8. *The Alarm Controls dialog box.*

Early Ring lets you specify the number of minutes prior
to the specified time that you want the alarm to ring. *Sound*
is a check box that lets you enable or disable the
audible alarm.

NOTE: *If the alarm is to be audible, Calendar must be running as either a Window or an icon.*

At the scheduled time, Calendar beeps (if sound is enabled)
and then notifies you of the alarm in one of the following
ways:

■ If Calendar is the active window, Calendar displays a
   reminder dialog box.

■ If Calendar is a nonactive window, Calendar's title
   bar blinks. Activate Calendar's window to display the
   reminder dialog box.

■ If Calendar is an icon, the icon blinks. Expand the icon
   to display the reminder dialog box.

NOTE: *If you are running a non-Windows application when
the alarm sounds, Calendar cannot notify you of the alarm until the application completes.*

Calendar's Monthly Planner

From a monthly calendar you can select a specific day and
view the day's appointments by double-clicking on the day
or by highlighting the day with the arrow keys and pressing
Enter.

Moving to Another Month

To move to a previous or future month, click on the arrows that appear in the time and date line, or press Ctrl+PgUp (previous month) or Ctrl+PgDn (following month).

Keyboard Combinations

The following table briefly summarizes Calendar's keyboard combinations:

Keyboard Combination	Function
F8	Selects the daily planner
F9	Selects the monthly planner
F4	Moves to a specific day's appointments
Ctrl+PgUp	Selects the previous day or month
Ctrl+PgDn	Selects the following day or month
F5	Sets or removes an alarm
F6	Marks a special day on the monthly planner
F7	Inserts a unique time (not necessarily an interval of 15, 30, or 60 minutes) on the daily planner
F1	Opens Calendar's online help

NOTE: *Calendar obtains the current date and time from your computer's internal clock. If the date and time are incorrect, use the Date/Time application in the Control Panel to reset them.*

CARDFILE

Cardfile lets you organize information on electronic ''index cards.'' These cards can store a list of names and addresses, birthdays, phone numbers, or any other type of information.

Starting Cardfile

Choose the Cardfile icon from the Accessories group. You'll see a window similar to the one shown in Figure 4-9.

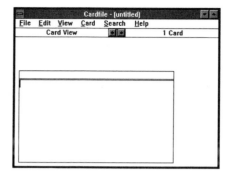

FIGURE 4-9. *A new Cardfile window.*

Creating a New Set of Cards

If you are creating a new set of cards, simply start typing to fill in the card's lower section.

Assigning an Index

The card's top line is the *index*. To assign an index to a card, follow these steps:

1. Double-click on the card's index line, or select Index from the Edit menu. You'll see the Index dialog box.

2. Type in a meaningful and—ideally—unique index name that describes the card, and then choose OK.

Adding a Card

To add a card, follow these steps:

1. Choose Add from the Card menu. You'll see the Add dialog box.

2. Type in a meaningful and—ideally—unique index name that describes the card's eventual contents, and then choose OK.

3. When Cardfile displays the card, type in the card's contents.

Saving Cards

To save your cards, follow these steps:

1. Choose Save As from the File menu. You'll see the File Save As dialog box.

2. Type in the desired filename. If you specify the name of an existing file, Cardfile displays a dialog box asking if you want to replace the existing file. Note that if you choose Yes, you lose the information in the existing file.

The File Menu

The following table briefly describes Cardfile's File menu:

Option	Function
New	Starts a new list of cards, asking if you want to save changes to the current card list
Open	Displays a dialog box that lets you load an existing card file
Save	Saves the list of cards to an existing file
Save As	Lets you save a list of cards with a new name
Print	Prints the current card
Print All	Prints every card in the list
Merge	Combines the current list of cards with another card file

Looking Through Your Cards

Cardfile gives you several ways to look through your cards.

Moving Forward and Backward

To move forward or backward through the list, click on the arrows in the Cardview line, or use one of the key combinations listed in the following table:

Key Combination	Movement
PgUp	Moves one card forward
PgDn	Moves one card backward
Ctrl+Home	Moves to the first card in the list
Ctrl+End	Moves to the last card in the list

Moving with the Index

You can click on the index of any card you want to see, or you can hold down the Ctrl key and type the first letter of the card's index name. If two index names begin with the same first letter, the card that has the index name that alphabetically comes first is displayed. Pressing the same key combination displays the second card.

Moving with the View Menu

Choose List from the View menu to display the cards as a list of scrollable index names. Cardfile always lists cards alphabetically by index name.

Moving with the Search Menu

Cardfile's Search menu provides two ways to search for a card: You can search by index name or by keyword.

Searching by index name. To search a set of cards for a specific index name, follow these steps:

1. Choose Go To from the Search menu. You'll see the Go To dialog box.

2. Type in the desired index name, and choose OK.

If Cardfile locates a matching index name, the matching card appears at the top of the deck. A dialog box informs you if no match is found.

Searching by keyword. To search through the text of the cards for a matching word or phrase, follow these steps:

1. Choose Find from the Search menu. You'll see the Find dialog box.

2. Type in the text you want to search for, and choose OK.

If Cardfile locates a card with matching text, the card containing the match appears at the top of the deck. If— despite the match—this is not the desired card, you can continue the search by pressing F3. A dialog box informs you if no match is found.

Editing Cards

To change a card's contents, follow these steps:

1. Select the desired card.

2. Use the arrow, Del, and Backspace keys to delete and insert text as necessary.

Changing a Card's Index Name

To change a card's index name, follow these steps:

1. Select the desired card.

2. Choose Index from the Edit menu, and type in a new index name.

Deleting a Card

To delete a card, follow these steps:

1. Select the desired card.

2. Choose Delete from the Card menu.

3. You'll see a dialog box asking you to confirm the deletion. Choose OK to delete the card, or Cancel to terminate the procedure.

Selecting Text

To select text, follow these steps:

 Position the mouse pointer over the start of the text, hold down the left mouse button, and then drag the mouse pointer to the end of the text. Release the left mouse button.

 Move the cursor to the beginning of the text, hold down the Shift key, and then use the arrow keys to move the cursor to the end of the text. Release the Shift key.

Copying Text from One Card to Another

To copy text from one card to another, follow these steps:

1. Select the desired card, and then select the desired text.

2. Choose Copy from the Edit menu.

3. Select the card to which you want to copy text. Move the cursor to the location where you want the text.

4. Choose Paste from the Edit menu.

Undoing an Editing Change

To undo an editing change, choose Restore from the Edit menu.

CLOCK

The most straightforward application is Clock. Clock displays the current time, using either an analog clock or a digital clock, as shown in Figure 4-10.

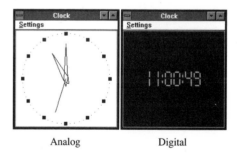

Analog   Digital

FIGURE 4-10. *The Clock window.*

The first time you start Clock you'll see an analog clock. To select the digital clock, choose Digital from the Settings menu. To change back to an analog clock, choose Analog from the Settings menu. When you change the clock type, the new type remains in effect—even if you leave Windows—until you specifically change it.

You can select the digital clock and then minimize Clock's window to an icon, displaying the current time at the bottom of the screen. This arrangement gives you constant access to the clock but leaves you free to work with other Windows applications.

NOTE: *Clock obtains the current time from your computer's internal clock. If the time is incorrect, use the Date/Time application in the Control Panel to reset it.*

NOTEPAD

Notepad is a simple text editor that lets you create memos, record notes, or create batch files.

NOTE: *The maximum size of a Notepad document is 55,000 characters.*

Starting Notepad

To start Notepad, expand the Notepad icon from the Accessories group. You'll see a window similar to the one in Figure 4-11.

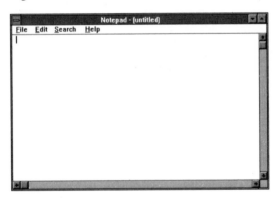

FIGURE 4-11. *A new Notepad window.*

Opening a Document

If you want to load an existing document, follow these steps:

1. Choose Open from the File menu. You'll see the File Open dialog box.

2. Type in the name of the document you want to open, or select it (and its directory, if necessary) from the Files and Directories list boxes. Then choose OK.

Creating a New Document

To create a new document, choose New from the File menu. (If you've made changes to the current document, a dialog box appears, asking whether you want to save the changes.)

Saving a Document

To save a document, choose Save from the File menu. If this is the first time you've saved the file, you'll see the File Save As dialog box. Simply type in the desired file name. (If a file with that name already exists, a dialog box asks whether you want to replace the existing file. If you choose Yes, the information in the existing file is lost.)

Notepad's File Menu

The following list briefly describes the menu items available in the File menu:

Menu Item	Function
New	Creates a new document, first prompting you to save or discard any changes to the current document
Open	Displays a dialog box that lets you load an existing document
Save	Saves the current document
Save As	Saves the current document with a new name
Print	Prints the document
Exit	Closes the Notepad window

Notepad Notes

■ By default, Notepad does not wrap text, so you must press Enter at the end of each line. (To have Notepad perform word wrapping, choose Word Wrap from the Edit menu.)

■ To move through a document, use the arrow, PgUp, PgDn, Home, and End keys, or the vertical and horizontal scroll bars if you're using a mouse.

The following table lists keyboard combinations that help you move around the screen:

Keyboard combination	Function
Home	Moves the cursor to the start of the current line
End	Moves the cursor to the end of the current line
Ctrl+Home	Moves the cursor to the start of the document
Ctrl+End	Moves the cursor to the end of the document
PgUp	Moves the cursor up one page
PgDn	Moves the cursor down one page
Ctrl+Right Arrow	Moves the cursor right one word
Ctrl+Left Arrow	Moves the cursor left one word

NOTE: *Notepad does not create a backup file for documents. When you save a changed document, the previous document is lost.*

Advanced File Editing

The following table describes the menu items available in the Edit menu.

Menu Item	Function
Undo	Cancels the most recent edit
Cut	Deletes the selected text and places it in the *clipboard*
Copy	Copies the selected text from the file to the clipboard
Paste	Copies the contents of the clipboard to the current document at the cursor's location
Delete	Removes the selected text from the document without placing the text in the clipboard
Select All	Selects all of the document's text
Time/Date	Inserts the date at the cursor location
Word Wrap	Enables word wrapping at right edge of the window

Moving Text

To move text to a different location in the document, follow these steps:

1. Select the desired text, and choose Cut from the Edit menu. The text disappears from your screen.

2. Move the cursor to where you want the text to reappear, and choose Paste from the Edit menu. The text reappears at the cursor location.

Searching for a Word or a Phrase

To search a document for a word or phrase, follow these steps.

1. Choose Find from the Search menu. You'll see a dialog box similar to Figure 4-12.

FIGURE 4-12. *The Find dialog box.*

2. Type in the text to search for.

3. Select the Match Upper/Lowercase check box if Notepad must match uppercase and lowercase letters exactly.

4. Select the direction you want Notepad to search (forward toward the end of the document or backward toward the beginning of the document).

If the search is successful, you'll see the desired portion of text on your screen. A dialog box informs you if no match occurs. If a match occurs but is *not* the match you want, press F3 to continue the search.

Controlling Notepad's Printed Output

If you choose Page Setup from Notepad's File menu, you'll see a dialog box similar to the one shown in Figure 4-13. This dialog box lets you specify a *header* (a line of text that appears at the top of each page) and a *footer* (a line of text that appears at the bottom of each page). This dialog box also lets you specify the page's margin sizes (in inches).

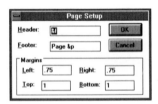

FIGURE 4-13. *The Page Setup dialog box.*

Creating a Time-Log Document

If the first line of your document contains the characters *.LOG* (capital letters required), Notepad creates a *time-log* document. Each time you open a time-log document, Notepad appends the current time and date to the end of the document. If you start your new text after the time and date, you will have a log of your work. Using the Search menu, you can quickly find a specific day's work.

To use the Page Setup dialog box, simply fill in the fields as desired, and then choose OK.

Customizing Your Headers

Place the following special characters in either the header or footer text to enhance your printed output:

Character Code	Function
&l	Flushes the header or the footer to the left margin
&r	Flushes the header or the footer to the right margin
&c	Centers the header or the footer
&d	Includes the date in the header or the footer
&f	Includes the document name in the header or the footer
&p	Includes page numbers in the header or the footer
&t	Includes the time in the header or the footer

PAINTBRUSH

Paintbrush lets you create your own graphics images or enhance graphics images created by a scanner.

NOTE: *If you try to use Paintbrush without a mouse, you'll quickly become frustrated. Accordingly, this section focuses on mouse operations. For more information on keyboard combinations—and for a detailed description of the Paintbrush program—see* Windows 3 Companion *(Microsoft Press, 1990).*

Starting Paintbrush

To start Paintbrush, choose the Paintbrush icon from the Accessories group. After you start Paintbrush, you'll see a window similar to the one in Figure 4-14.

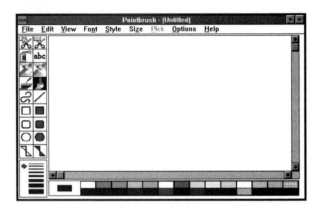

FIGURE 4-14. *A new Paintbrush window.*

Using the File Menu

The following list describes the menu items available in
Paintbrush's File menu:

Menu Item	Function
New	Creates a new image, first prompting you to save or discard any changes to the current image
Open	Displays a dialog box that lets you load an existing image
Save	Saves the current image
Save As	Saves the current image with a new name
Page Setup	Lets you assign headers, footers, and margins
Print	Prints the current image
Printer Setup	Configures the printer
Exit	Closes the Paintbrush window

Paintbrush provides a collection of drawing tools described here:

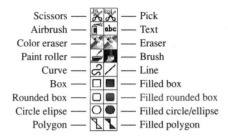

Scissors —	— Pick
Airbrush —	— Text
Color eraser —	— Eraser
Paint roller —	— Brush
Curve —	— Line
Box —	— Filled box
Rounded box —	— Filled rounded box
Circle elipse —	— Filled circle/ellipse
Polygon —	— Filled polygon

Tool	Function
Scissors	Cuts a free-form portion of the image to move or delete
Pick	Cuts a rectangular portion of the image to move or delete
Airbrush	Spray-paints the image with the current color
Text Tool	Places text into the image
Color Eraser	Erases areas of the current color
Erase	Erases areas of any color
Paint roller	Fills an area with the current color
Brush	Paints using the current color
Curve	Draws a smooth curved line
Line	Draws a straight line
Box	Draws an unfilled rectangle
Filled Box	Draws a rectangle filled with the current color
Rounded Box	Draws an unfilled rectangle with rounded corners
Filled Rounded Box	Draws a rectangle with rounded edges filled with the current color
Circle/Ellipse	Draws an unfilled ellipse
Filled Circle/ Ellipse	Draws an ellipse filled with the current color
Polygon	Draws an unfilled irregular shape
Filled Polygon	Draws an irregular shape filled with the current color

Selecting a Tool

To select a tool, simply click on the tool.

Selecting Line Thickness

Below the Paintbrush tool set are eight horizontal lines of varying thickness. You use these lines to define the thickness Paintbrush uses to draw or erase lines and shapes. To change the thickness, simply click on the desired thickness.

Selecting Colors

To the right of the line-size box is the color palette, along with the foreground and background color indicator. To select a foreground color, simply click (using the left mouse button) on the desired color. To select a background color, click (using the right mouse button) on the desired color.

NOTE: *If you have swapped the functions of the mouse buttons, as described in Part III, you'll use the right button to select the foreground color and the left button to select the background color.*

Working with Your Image

The following tips should prove helpful as you begin to create and work with Paintbrush images:

■ If your image becomes larger than the canvas area, use the horizontal and vertical scroll bars to view different parts of the image.

■ Choose Zoom In from the View menu to temporarily magnify a portion of the image to allow detailed editing. (While you're zoomed in, you edit pixel-by-pixel with each click of the mouse.) When you've finished with the detailed editing, choose Zoom Out from the View menu to restore the image to its normal size.

Using the Paintbrush Tools

The following sections briefly describe the use of each
Paintbrush tool.

Working with the Scissors Tool

The Scissors tool lets you cut out an irregularly shaped
area. (After creating this ''cutout,'' you can perform a
variety of operations on it. See ''Fun with Cutouts'' later in
this section.)

To use the Scissors tool, follow these steps:

1. Select the Scissors tool. The mouse pointer changes to a
   cross hair.

2. Place the mouse pointer on the starting point of the area
   to select.

3. Hold down the mouse button, and then draw around the
   area you want to select. When you've completely encircled the area, release the mouse button.

Working with the Pick Tool

The Pick tool provides a convenient way to cut out a rectangular area. (After creating such a ''cutout,'' you can perform a variety of operations on it. See ''Fun with Cutouts''
later in this section.)

To use the Pick tool, follow these steps:

1. Select the Pick tool. The mouse pointer changes to a
   cross hair.

2. Place the mouse pointer at the upper left corner of the
   rectangular area you want to select.

3. Hold down the mouse button, and then move the mouse
   pointer to create a rectangular border around the desired
   area. Then release the mouse button.

Erasing Areas

Paintbrush's Color Eraser tool and Eraser tool let you erase
areas of the image. The Color Eraser, however, only erases
text or graphics of the selected foreground color replacing
it with the background color. The selected line size affects

how much area the erasers remove at one time. A thick line erases more area, whereas a thin line gives you finer control.

To erase an area, follow these steps:

1. Select either the Color Eraser tool or the Eraser tool. The mouse pointer changes to a cross hair inside a square. If you've selected the Color Eraser tool, select the color to erase.

2. Move the mouse pointer to the area you want to erase.

3. Hold down the mouse button, and then drag the mouse to erase the area.

4. When you've finished erasing, release the mouse button.

Fun with Cutouts

Cutouts can be treated in a variety of different ways. The following list provides a simple description of the operations available. Experiment! Or, for further information, see *Windows 3 Companion* (Microsoft Press, 1990).

Operation	Description
Cut	Removes the cutout from the window and places it in the clipboard.
Copy	Places a copy of the cutout in the clipboard.
Paste	Pastes a copy of the clipboard into the window.
Flip Horizontal	Reverses the cutout horizontally.
Flip Vertical	Reverses the cutout vertically.
Inverse	Inverts the cutout colors. (Look at the bottom of the window. You'll see two rows of colors. The bottom colors are the *inverse* of the top colors and vice versa.)
Shrink + Grow	Allows you to copy and size a cutout.
Tilt	Allows you to copy and skew a cutout.
Clear	Changes the background area within the original cutout to the background color when you choose Shrink + Grow or Tilt.

Working with the Airbrush

The Airbrush tool works like a can of spray paint, letting you shade areas. By selecting different line sizes and colors, you can change the Airbrush tool's effect.

To use the Airbrush tool, follow these steps:

1. Select the Airbrush tool. The mouse pointer will change to a cross hair.

2. Select a color.

3. Press the mouse button to airbrush an area. Hold down the mouse button, and drag the mouse to airbrush a large area. Release the mouse button to shut the airbrush off. By concentrating the airbrush in an area, you can create darker shades.

Adding Text to an Image

Many images you create will need labels, titles, or other text. The Text tool lets you add text to an image. Depending on your image, you will want to select an appropriate font, font size, and text attribute such as bold, italic, or underlined. The Font, Style and Size menus let you do just that.

To add text to your image, follow these steps.

1. Select the Text tool. The mouse pointer changes to an I-beam.

2. Select the color you'd like the text to be.

3. Select a font from the Font menu.

4. Select a font style from the Style menu.

5. Select a font size from the Size menu.

6. Click on the location where you'd like the text to appear. Type in the desired text.

Using the Paint Roller

The Paint Roller lets you fill a bordered area with the selected color. If the border has an opening, the color leaks through the border, filling outer areas.

To use the Paint Roller, follow these steps:

1. Select the Paint Roller tool. The mouse pointer changes to look like a paint roller.

2. Select the desired color.

3. Move the mouse pointer to (inside) the area you'd like filled, and press the mouse button.

Using the Brush

The Brush tool lets you draw using the selected color and line thickness. To use the Brush tool, follow these steps:

1. Select the Brush tool. The mouse pointer changes to a square.

2. Select the desired color.

3. Select the desired line thickness. The size of the mouse pointer changes to reflect your choice.

4. Move the mouse pointer to the desired location. Hold down the mouse button, and move the mouse to draw.

5. When you've finished drawing, release the mouse button.

Drawing Lines

The Curve tool and the Line tool let you draw curved or straight lines. To create a straight line, follow these steps:

1. Select the Line tool. The mouse pointer changes to a cross hair.

2. Select the desired color.

3. Select the desired line thickness.

4. Click where you want the line to begin, and drag the mouse to create the desired shape. Then release the mouse button.

To draw a curved line, follow these steps:

1. Select the Curve tool. The mouse pointer changes to a cross hair.

2. Select the desired color.

3. Select the desired line thickness.

4. Click where you want the line to begin, and drag the mouse to create the desired shape. Then release the mouse button.

5. Next hold down the mouse button and drag. The line curves to follow the mouse pointer. When the line is in the desired shape, release the mouse button. If you're satisfied with the shape, click on the second endpoint to finalize the curve. If you want to add a second curve to the line, click and drag again.

Drawing Boxes

Paintbrush lets you draw four types of boxes: empty boxes, empty boxes with rounded corners, filled boxes, and filled boxes with rounded corners. (The border of a filled box is drawn with the selected background color, and then filled with the selected foreground color.)

To draw a box, follow these steps:

1. Select the desired box tool. The cursor changes to a cross hair.

2. Select the desired foreground color. For a filled rectangle, also select a background color.

3. Select the desired line thickness.

4. Move the mouse pointer to the location where you want the box to appear. Drag the mouse to create the desired shape, and then release the mouse button.

Creating Circles and Ellipses

Paintbrush lets you create empty or filled circles and ellipses. An *ellipse* is simply an elongated circle. (The border of a filled circle or ellipse is drawn with the selected background color and then filled with the selected foreground color.)

To draw a circle or an ellipse, follow these steps:

1. Select the desired circle/ellipse tool. The cursor changes to a cross hair.

2. Select the desired foreground color. For a filled circle or ellipse, also select a background color.

3. Select the desired line thickness.

4. Move the mouse pointer to the location where you want the circle or ellipse to be. Drag the mouse to create the desired shape, and then release the mouse button. (You'll have the tendency to create an ellipse. If you want to ensure that you draw a true circle, press Shift before you release the mouse button.)

Creating Polygons

A *polygon* is an irregularly shaped closed object. Paint-brush lets you create empty and filled polygons. To create a polygon, follow these steps:

1. Select a polygon tool. The mouse pointer changes to a cross hair.

2. Select the desired foreground color. For a filled polygon, also select a background color.

3. Select the desired line thickness.

4. Move the mouse pointer to the location of the first corner of the border of the polygon and click.

5. Move the mouse pointer to the location of the second corner of the border of the polygon and click. A line appears between the first and second corners.

6. Move the mouse pointer to the location of the next corner of the border of the polygon and click. A line appears between the second and third corners. Repeat this process for each corner of the polygon. Finish the polygon by clicking on the starting point.

RECORDER

As you work with Windows on a regular basis, you might find yourself repeatedly opening the same windows and running the same applications. To save time and key-strokes, you can create Windows *macros*. A Windows macro is a record of the keystrokes and mouse operations required to perform a certain task. The Recorder application lets you record the keystrokes and mouse operations you perform on a regular basis to a macro. When you later need to perform the operation, you can run the macro to perform the steps automatically.

Starting Recorder

To start Recorder, expand the Recorder icon from the Accessories Group. You'll see a window similar to Figure 4-15.

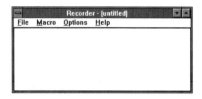

FIGURE 4-15. *A new Recorder window.*

Recording a Macro

Normally, you use the mouse to select and choose options. However, this can cause problems in a macro because options such as menus, check boxes, and radio buttons aren't always in the same place. To avoid this problem, it's wise to use keyboard combinations rather than the mouse when selecting and choosing options to be recorded as a Windows macro.

To record a Windows macro, follow these steps:

1. Choose Record from the Macro menu. You'll see a dialog box similar to the one in Figure 4-16.

2. Type in a descriptive macro name, but do *not* press Enter.

3. Move to the Shortcut Key box, and select a shortcut (keyboard) combination you want to use to run the macro. For example, if you want the keyboard combination Ctrl+Alt+T to run this macro, type T in the Shortcut Key text box, and then select the Ctrl and Alt check boxes. (Do not select a keyboard combination that conflicts with the application your macro assists.)

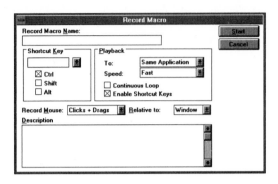

FIGURE 4-16. *The Record Macro dialog box.*

4. The default selections for the remaining options should be fine. You might want to include a description of the macro's processing in the Description box.

5. Choose Start to begin recording. The Recorder window becomes a blinking icon to indicate that the recording process has begun.

6. Perform the operations you want to record.

7. When you are finished performing the operations you want to record, expand the Recorder icon. You'll see a dialog box similar to the one in Figure 4-17.

FIGURE 4-17. *The Recorder dialog box.*

8. Select Save Macro, and choose OK.

Saving a Macro

To save a macro on disk, follow these steps:

1. Choose Save As from the File menu. You'll see a dialog box that lets you specify a filename.

2. Type in a filename, and choose OK. If a file with that name already exists, Recorder displays a second dialog box asking whether you want to replace the existing file. Choose yes to replace it or no to cancel the operation.

Loading a Macro

To load a macro, follow these steps:

1. Choose Open from the File menu. You'll see a dialog box asking for the name of the macro file.

2. Type in the macro filename and choose OK. Recorder shows the names of each macro in the file.

Running a Macro

To run a macro, Recorder must be running, and the macro must be loaded. To run a macro, press the macro's keyboard combination.

Other Recorder Options

Select or deselect the following menu items to control how Recorder operates:

Menu Item	Function
Control+Break Checking	When enabled, allows Ctrl+Break or Ctrl+C to stop a Windows macro
Shortcut Keys	When enabled, allows use of keyboard combinations with Windows macros
Minimize On Use	When enabled, reduces the Recorder to an icon when a Windows macro is run

TERMINAL

Terminal is a telecommunications application that lets one computer exchange information with another, typically via phone lines.

Starting Terminal

To start Terminal, expand the Terminal icon from the Accessories group. You'll see a window similar to the one in Figure 4-18.

FIGURE 4-18. *A new Terminal window.*

Identifying Your Modem

Terminal needs to know what type of modem you are using. To provide this information, follow these steps:

1. Choose Modem Commands from the Settings menu. You'll see a dialog box similar to the one in Figure 4-19.

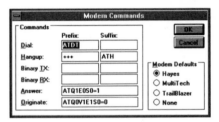

FIGURE 4-19. *The Modem Commands dialog box.*

2. If your modem is listed in the Modem Defaults box, select the option button that corresponds to it. If your modem is not listed, select the Hayes option button.

3. Select the Prefix field of the Dial command text box. The letters *ATDT* tell the modem your phone uses touch-tone dialing. If your phone is rotary based, change these letters to *ATDP*. The remaining command options in this dialog box are fairly standard, and you should not have to change them unless explicitly directed by your modem documentation.

4. Choose OK.

Setting Up Communication Parameters

Before two computers can communicate, they must agree on a set of communication parameters, such as communication speeds and settings. If you access several different computers, each might use a unique set of data communication parameters. To set these up appropriately, follow these steps:

1. Choose Communications from the Settings menu. You'll see a dialog box similar to the one in Figure 4-20.

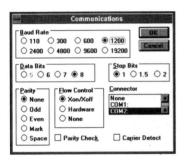

FIGURE 4-20. *The Communications dialog box.*

2. Select the data communication settings used by the computer you'll be calling. (You'll need to find this out from the owner of the other computer.)

Setting Up a Phone Number

You must specify the phone number of the computer you want to call. To do so, follow these steps:

1. Choose Phone Number from the Settings menu. You'll see a dialog box similar to the one in Figure 4-21.

FIGURE 4-21. *The Phone Number dialog box.*

2. Type in the number of the computer you intend to call. Type it in as you would dial it. (That is, if you must dial 9 to access an outside line, include the 9 in the Dial field. If the phone call is long distance, include a 1 and the area code.) You can separate digits with spaces, parentheses, or hyphens. A comma directs the modem to pause two seconds before continuing dialing. (This is useful to give an office phone system time to connect with an outside line.)

The remaining fields let you tell Terminal what steps to perform if a modem at the other end of the phone line fails to respond in the specified time period:

☐ Timeout if Not Connected In lets you specify how long the computer should try to make a connection. Depending on how far you are calling and on the number of times the phone rings before the other modem answers, you might need to increase the timeout period to 60 seconds.

☐ Redial After Timing Out lets you direct Terminal to keep recalling until it connects to the other computer.

☐ Signal when Connected directs Terminal to beep to notify you of the connection when it successfully connects to the other computer.

3. When you've finished setting options, choose OK.

Saving Communications Information

To save the communications information, choose Save As from the File Menu. You'll see a dialog box asking you for a filename. Type in a filename, and choose OK. (Unless you specify otherwise, Terminal saves the file with a .TRM filename extension.)

Loading Communications Information

To load the communications information back into Terminal, choose Open from the File Menu. You'll see a dialog box asking what file to load. Type in the filename, or select the filename (and directory, if necessary) from the Files and Directories list boxes. Then choose OK.

Placing a Phone Call

After you've assigned the data communications settings and phone number, you're ready to place a call. To do so, follow these steps:

1. Choose Dial from the Phone menu. You'll see a dialog box that displays the phone number being called, as well as a countdown of seconds until timeout. If Terminal successfully reaches the other modem, you might hear the two modems exchange tones as they form a connection.

2. When the tones complete, press Enter to begin your interaction with the other computer.

3. To end the connection, choose Hangup from the Phone menu. Terminal directs your modem to disconnect the call and hangs up the line.

Transferring Files

One of the primary reasons for connecting your computer to another computer is to exchange files. In general, the files you exchange are either text (ASCII files created by a text editor such as Notepad) or binary files such as programs, spreadsheets, or word processing files. Terminal lets you send and receive both kinds of files.

Sending Files

To send a file to another computer, follow these steps. (The other computer must be prepared to receive a file.)

1. To send a text file, choose Send Text File from the Transfers menu. To send a binary file, choose Send Binary File from the Transfers menu.

2. Type in the name of the file you want to send, and choose OK.

You'll see a small status bar at the bottom of the window that lets you monitor the transfer:

- If Terminal successfully transfers the file, the status bar disappears, and interactive mode resumes.

- If an error occurs during transmission, you'll see a dialog box describing the error. You might need to set a Text Transfer or Binary Transfer setting. For more information on these settings, use Terminal's online help, or refer to *Windows 3 Companion* (Microsoft Press, 1990).

Receiving Files

To receive a file, follow these steps:

1. Choose Receive Text File from Terminal's Transfers menu. You'll see a dialog box prompting you for the name of the file to receive the text. (You can optionally append the text to an existing file.)

2. Type in the filename, and press Enter. You'll see all text from the remote computer scroll by on the screen as Terminal captures it in the file. A status bar at the bottom of the window lets you monitor the number of bytes transferred.

3. To end the transmission, click on the Stop button, or choose Stop from Terminal's Transfer menu. If an error occurs, a dialog box describing the error appears.

WRITE

Write is a word processing application that lets you create and edit professional-quality letters and reports. Beyond performing the normal editing tasks of cutting and pasting text, Write lets you align paragraphs, use different character fonts, and even integrate graphics images you create with Paintbrush.

Starting Write

To start Write, expand Write's icon from the Accessories group. You'll see a window similar to the one in Figure 4-22.

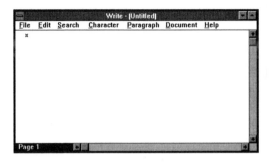

FIGURE 4-22. *A new Write window.*

Opening an Existing Document

To open an existing document, choose Open from Write's File menu. You'll see the File Open dialog box. Type in the name of the file, or select the filename (and directory, if necessary) from the Files: and Directories: list boxes. Then choose OK.

Creating a New Document

To create a new document, choose New from the File menu. If you've made any changes to the current document, Write first asks if you want to save the changes to the current document.

Saving a Document

After you complete the document, you need to save it on a file on disk. To do so, choose Save from Write's File menu. The following list briefly describes the items in Write's File menu.

Menu Item	Function
New	Creates a new document, first asking if you want to save any changes to the current document
Open	Lets you load an existing document
Save	Saves a document
Save As	Saves a document with a new name
Print	Prints the document
Printer Setup	Configures the printer
Repaginate	Verifies current page breaks before printing
Exit	Closes the Write window

Moving Through Your Document

You can move to a different area in your document by using either the mouse or the keyboard.

1. To move up or down one line at a time, click on the up or down arrow in the scroll bar.

2. To move up or down one screen at a time, click on the scroll bar above or below the scroll box.

3. To rapidly move to a new area, drag the scroll box up or down.

Figure 4-23 shows the key combinations used to move to a different area of your document:

Keyboard Combination	Cursor Movement
Home	Moves the cursor to the start of the current line
End	Moves the cursor to the end of the current line
Ctrl+Home	Moves the cursor to the start of the document
Ctrl+End	Moves the cursor to the end of the document
PgUp	Moves the cursor up one page
PgDn	Moves the cursor down one page
Ctrl+PgUp	Moves the cursor to the top of the page

FIGURE 4-23. *Write's cursor-movement keyboard* *(continued)*
combinations.

Keyboard
Combination **Cursor Movement**

Ctrl+PgDn	Moves the cursor to the bottom of the page
Ctrl+Right Arrow	Moves the cursor right one word
Ctrl+Left Arrow	Moves the cursor left one word
Goto+Right Arrow*	Moves the cursor to the next sentence
Goto+Left Arrow*	Moves the cursor to the previous sentence
Goto+Down Arrow*	Moves the cursor to the next paragraph
Goto+Up Arrow*	Moves the cursor to the previous paragraph
Goto+PgDn*	Moves the cursor to the next page, according to the last repagination
Goto+PgUp*	Moves the cursor to the previous page, according to the last repagination

*Goto represents the numeric keypad 5 key.

Editing Your Document

Write lets you move, copy, or delete sections of your document. To use Write's edit menu, you must first select the text. To do so, follow these steps:

Position the mouse pointer over the start of the text, hold down the mouse button, and then drag the mouse pointer to the last of the text you want to select. Then release the mouse button.

Move the cursor to the beginning of the text, hold down the Shift key, and then use the arrow keys to move the cursor to the end of the text you want to select. Then release the Shift key.

Moving Text

To move text from one location to another, follow these steps:

1. Select the text to move, and then choose Cut from the Edit menu.

2. Move the cursor to the location in the document where you want the text, and then choose Paste from the Edit menu.

Copying Text

To copy text from one location to another, follow these steps:

1. Select the text to copy, and then choose Copy from the Edit menu.

2. Move the cursor to the location in the document to which you want to copy the text. Choose Paste from Write's Edit menu. Repeat this step at each location to which you want to copy the text.

Deleting Text

To delete text, simply select the text, and choose Cut from the Edit menu.

Cutting and Pasting Graphics

Write lets you Paste graphics images into a document from the clipboard. To place a graphics image you have created using Paintbrush (such as a logo) into your Write document, follow these steps:

1. Within Paintbrush, use the Scissors tool or the Pick tool to place the image in the clipboard. (See ''Paintbrush,'' earlier in this section.)

2. Activate the Write window, and open the document in which the image is to be placed.

3. Move to the location in the document where you want the image to appear. Choose Paste from the Edit menu.

Sizing an image. After you place the image into the document, you can resize it to suit your needs. To resize an image, follow these steps:

1. Select the image:

 Click on the image.

 Move the cursor to the beginning of the image, hold down the Shift key, and then press the down arrow.

2. Choose Size Picture from the Edit menu. A box appears around the image.

3. Use the mouse or arrow keys to resize the box surrounding the image. When the box is the correct size, click the mouse or press Enter. The image is redrawn in the proper size.

Positioning an image. After you place the image into the document, you can move it to suit your needs. To move an image, follow these steps:

1. Select the image:

 Click on the image.

 Move the cursor to the beginning of the image, hold down the Shift key, and then press the down arrow.

2. Choose Move Picture from the Edit menu. A box appears around the image.

3. Use the mouse or arrow keys to move the box surrounding the image. When the box is positioned properly, click the mouse or press Enter. The image is redrawn in the new location.

Using the Search Menu

The Search menu provides several ways of moving through a document.

Searching for Text

To search your document for a string of text, follow these steps:

1. Choose Find from Write's Search menu. You'll see a dialog box similar to the one in Figure 4-24.

FIGURE 4-24. *The Find dialog box.*

2. Type in the text you are searching for.

3. Select Whole Word if you want Write to distinguish the text from words containing the text (for example, if you want to find the word book and want to ignore the word bookmark).

4. Select Match Upper/Lowercase if Write must match uppercase and lowercase letters exactly (for example, if you want to find Book but not book).

5. Choose Find Next. If Write finds the text in the document, it displays the part of the document containing the text; otherwise, Write displays a dialog box telling you the text was not found.

6. To search for another occurrence of the text, choose Find Next; otherwise, choose Close from the dialog box's Control menu.

Changing a Word or a Phrase

Write lets you quickly search for and change each occurrence of a word or a phrase throughout your document. To change a word or a phrase, follow these steps:

1. Move to the location in the document where you want the changes to begin.

2. Choose Change from the Search menu. You'll see a dialog box similar to Figure 4-25.

FIGURE 4-25. *The Change dialog box.*

3. In the Find What field, type the word or phrase to change, but do *not* press Enter. In the Change To field, type the desired word or phrase, but do *not* press Enter.

4. Select Whole Word if you want Write to distinguish the text from words containing the text (for example, if you want to find the word book and want to ignore the word bookmark).

5. Select Match Upper/Lowercase if Write must match uppercase and lowercase letters exactly (for example, if you want to find Book but not book).

6. Choose the Find button that best suits your needs:

Find Button	Result
Find Next	Finds the next match but doesn't change it
Change	Changes the current match
Change, then Find	Changes the current match and finds the next match
Change All	Changes all matching text, starting from the beginning of the document

Moving to a Specific Page

To move to a specific page in the document, follow these steps:

1. Choose Go To Page from the Search menu. You'll see a dialog box similar to the one in Figure 4-26.

FIGURE 4-26. *The Go To dialog box.*

2. Type in the number of the page you'd like to move to, and then choose OK.

Changing Character Fonts

Write provides several character fonts for use in your Write documents. Write gives you two ways to select and use fonts: You can select a specific font and type. (The text you type appears in the new font.) Or you can change any existing text to a new font. To do so, follow these steps:

1. Select the desired text.

2. Choose Fonts from the Character menu. You'll see a dialog box similar to Figure 4-27.

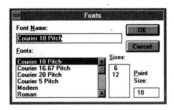

FIGURE 4-27. *The Fonts dialog box.*

3. Select a font from the Font list and a size from the Sizes list, and then choose OK.

Using the Character Menu

Write's Character menu lets you select fonts, font sizes, and text attributes such as bold, underline, or italic. Reduce Font and Enlarge Font incrementally decrease or increase a font size. If you select one of these items and no change appears on your screen, your printer does not support the selected font.

If you choose Fonts from Write's Character menu, you'll see a dialog box similar to Figure 4-27. Simply select the font and size you want to use, and choose OK.

Using the Paragraph Menu

Write automatically wraps text at the right edge of the window. The only time you need to press Enter is to distinguish one paragraph in your document from another. Write's Paragraph menu lets you specify paragraph alignment, line spacing within paragraphs, and paragraph indentation. The following list briefly describes the formatting options available from the Paragraph menu:

Menu Item	Function
Left	Justifies text along the left margin only
Centered	Centers text between left and right margins
Right	Justifies text along the right margin only
Justified	Justifies text along left and right margins
Single Space	Single-spaces a paragraph
1½ Space	Uses 1½ spaces between lines in a paragraph
Double Space	Double spaces a paragraph
Indents	Lets you set paragraph indents

NOTE: *If you have a mouse, you can set these paragraph values with the Ruler. See "Using the Document Ruler" later in this section.*

Changing Paragraph Justification

To change a paragraph's justification, follow these steps:

1. Place the cursor within the paragraph to justify.

2. Select the desired justification from the Paragraph menu.

Changing Paragraph Spacing

Write lets you single, double, or triple space the lines of text in a paragraph. To change a paragraph's spacing, follow these steps:

1. Place the cursor within the desired paragraph.

2. Select the desired spacing from the Paragraph menu.

Changing Paragraph Indentation

Write lets you indent a paragraph from the left and right margins. The first sentence can be indented separately to make it stand out. To indent a paragraph, follow these steps:

1. Place the cursor within the desired paragraph.

2. Choose Indents from the Paragraph menu. You'll see a dialog box similar to the one in Figure 4-28.

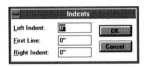

FIGURE 4-28. *The Indents dialog box.*

3. Type in the indentations you want, and then choose OK.

Formatting Your Document

Write's Document menu lets you control aspects of your entire document.

Adding a Header or a Footer

A *header* is text—such as a title, your name, or a page number—that appears at the top of each page throughout your document. Likewise, a *footer* is text that appears at the bottom of each page. To add a header or a footer to your document, follow these steps:

1. Choose Header or Footer from Write's Document menu. You'll see a window where you type in the actual text for the header or footer, along with a dialog box that lets you provide certain information *about* the text.

2. Type in the header or footer you want. When you're satisfied with the text, press Alt+F6 to move to the dialog box.

3. In the Distance from Top: field (if you're creating a footer, the field is Distance from Bottom:), specify a value—in inches—that dictates how far the header or footer falls from the top (header) or bottom (footer) of the page.

4. Select Print on First Page if you want your header or footer to appear on the first page.

5. Select Insert Page Number if you want page numbers to accompany your header or footer.

6. If you're happy with your choices, choose Return to Document. If you'd like to revise your header or footer, press Alt+F6 to move to the window and edit your header or footer text. Or, if you want to start from scratch, simply choose Clear to erase the header or footer, and press Alt+F6. Begin again at step 2, above.

Setting Tab Stops

By default, Write allows tab stops at every half inch. You can set up to 12 tab stops of your own. To do so, follow these steps.

NOTE: *If you have a mouse, you can set tabs with the document ruler. See "Using the Document Ruler" later in this section.*

1. Choose Tabs from Write's Document menu. You'll see a dialog box similar to the one in Figure 4-29.

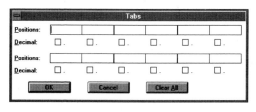

FIGURE 4-29. *The Tabs dialog box.*

2. Select an empty Positions box.

3. Type in the tab stop's distance from the left margin in inches (").

4. Select the corresponding Decimal box if you want to align decimal points in a column of numbers.

5. When you've finished setting tab stops, choose OK.

Deleting a Tab Stop

To delete a tab stop, follow these steps:

1. Choose Tabs from the Document menu.

2. Select the Positions box for the tab stop you want removed.

3. Use the Backspace key to delete the measurement.

4. When you've finished deleting tab stops, choose OK.

Using the Document Ruler

The *document ruler* is a line Write displays below its menu bar to help you view and control tab stops, margins, and indentation (Figure 4-30).

To toggle the ruler on and off, choose Ruler On/Off from the Document menu.

Setting Tabs with the Document Ruler

To set tabs with the document ruler follow these steps:

1. Click on the icon for the type of tab you want (normal or decimal).

2. Click in the ruler at the location where you want a tab to appear.

Setting Paragraph Spacing with the Document Ruler

To set paragraph spacing with the document ruler, follow these steps:

1. Click anywhere within the paragraph you want to format.

2. Click on the icon for the type of spacing you want.

Setting Paragraph Justification

To set paragraph justification with the document ruler, follow these steps:

1. Click anywhere within the paragraph you want to format.

2. Click on the icon for the type of justification you want.

Tab

Decimal tab

Single space

1 1/2 space

Double space

Left justify

Center

Right justify

Justify left and right

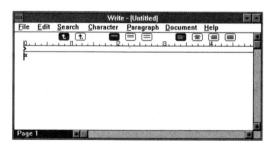

FIGURE 4-30. *The document ruler displays your screen measurements.*

Keyboard Combinations

The following list describes Write's keyboard combinations.

Keyboard Combination	Function
Shift+Del	Cuts selected text from the document and places it in the clipboard
Ctrl+Ins	Copies selected text to the clipboard
Shift+Ins	Pastes clipboard contents into the document at the cursor location
F3	Repeats the most recent Find operation
F4	Activates Goto page dialog box
Ctrl+B	Enables bold text
Ctrl+I	Enables italic text
Ctrl+U	Enables underlined text

THE PIF EDITOR

The more Windows knows about the way a program operates, the better Windows integrates that application into the Windows environment with the rest of your applications. Windows-based applications automatically supply Windows with the information it needs, but DOS-based applications do not.

A *PIF* is a Program Information File that provides Windows with key information it needs to know about non-Windows applications. In most cases, you don't need to create a PIF for every non-Windows application you use; Windows provides a default PIF which is normally sufficient. If you want to provide Windows with more specific information about a non-Windows application, however, you can create a PIF using the PIF Editor. Depending on your Windows mode, the steps you must perform—and the information you must provide—differ. In either mode, however, you perform the following operations.

Creating a PIF

To create a PIF for a non-Windows application, follow these steps:

1. Expand the PIF Editor icon in the Accessories group window.

2. Set all fields as desired. (Standard mode fields are covered in the section titled ''Real and Standard Mode.'' 386 enhanced fields are covered in the section titled ''386 Enhanced Mode.'')

3. After you complete all fields, choose Save As from the File menu. Type in a filename, and choose OK.

Editing an Existing PIF

To edit an existing PIF, follow these steps:

1. Choose Open from the File menu.

2. Type in the name of the file, or select the file using the Files: and Directories: list boxes.

3. Set all fields as desired. (Standard mode fields are covered in the section titled ''Real and Standard Mode.'' 386 enhanced fields are covered in the section titled ''386 Enhanced Mode.'')

4. Choose Save from the File menu.

Real and Standard Mode

When you run the PIF Editor in real or standard mode, you'll see a PIF Editor window similar to Figure 4-31.

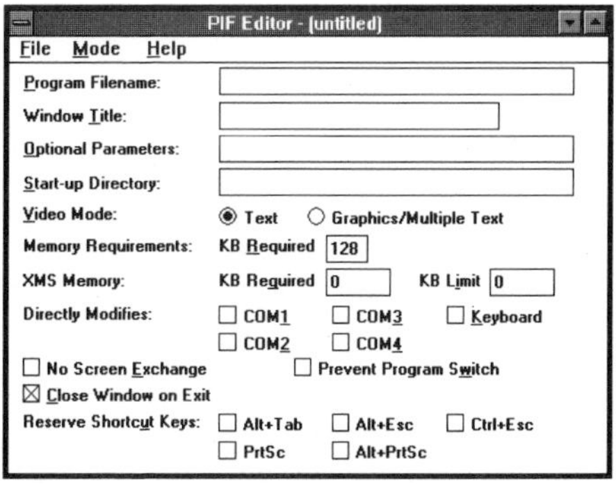

FIGURE 4-31. *A new PIF Editor window.*

The following paragraphs briefly describe each real and standard mode PIF field:

■ *Program Filename* specifies the application's complete pathname (drive, directory, filename, and extension). If the application is in your computer's search path, you need only enter the application's name.

■ *Window Title* specifies the name you want to appear in the application's title bar or beneath the application's icon when minimized. Typically, you should use the application's name.

■ *Optional Parameters* specifies the application's command line. If you use the question mark (?), Windows displays a dialog box before the application runs to prompt you for the command line.

■ *Start-up Directory* directs Windows to change to the directory specified before running the application. If you don't specify a directory, Windows uses the current directory.

■ *Video Mode* specifies the video mode the application runs in. If you are not sure of the video mode used, select Graphics/Multiple Text.

■ *Memory Requirements* tells Windows the minimum amount of memory (in KB) the application needs.

■ *XMS Memory* has two fields: KB Required and KB Limit. KB Required specifies the amount of extended memory (in KB) the application needs. KB Limit specifies the maximum amount of extended memory Windows should let the application use.

■ *Directly Modifies* tells Windows what devices the application modifies, letting Windows restrict the device's use by other applications.

■ *No Screen Exchange* prevents you from copying the application's screen into the Clipboard using PrtSc and Alt+PrtSc. The only reason to select this option is to provide a small amount of extra memory to the application.

- *Prevent Program Switch* lets Windows save a small amount of memory by preventing you from switching from this application to another. When this option is selected, you must exit the application to return to Windows.

- *Close Window on Exit* directs Windows to close the application's window when the application ends, as opposed to displaying the application's ending screen and prompting you with the message Hit Any Key To Exit.

- *Reserve Shortcut Keys* directs Windows to reserve the specified keyboard combinations for the application's use, instead of treating the keys as predefined Windows keyboard combinations.

386 Enhanced Mode

When you run the PIF Editor in 386 enhanced mode, you'll see a PIF Editor similar to Figure 4-32.

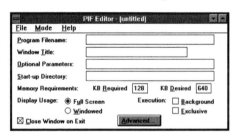

FIGURE 4-32. *A new PIF Editor window.*

The following paragraphs briefly describe each 386 enhanced mode PIF field:

- *Program Filename* specifies the application's complete pathname (drive, directory, filename, and extension). If the application is in your computer's search path, you need only enter the application's name.

- *Window Title* specifies the name you want to appear in the application's title bar or beneath the application's icon when minimized. Typically, you should use the application's name.

- *Optional Parameters* specifies the application's command line. If you use the question mark (?), Windows displays a dialog box before the application runs to prompt you for the command line.

- *Start-up Directory* directs Windows to change to the directory specified before running the application. If you don't specify a directory, Windows uses the current directory.

- *Memory Requirements* has two fields: KB Required and KB Desired. KB Required specifies the minimum amount of memory the application needs. KB Desired specifies the maximum amount of memory Windows should let the application use. The only reason to change this entry is to reserve more memory for other applications.

- *Display Usage* has two option buttons: Full Screen and Windowed. Full Screen specifies that the application should run full screen, while Windowed specifies that the application should be run in a window. Windows lets you toggle an application's display between full screen and a window by pressing Alt+Enter.

- *Execution* contains two check boxes: Background and Exclusive. If you select Background, Windows allows the application to run in the background while you use another application. If you deselect Background, Windows stops running the application when you switch to another application. Selecting Exclusive tells Windows to suspend execution of all other applications while the application controlled by this PIF is running in the foreground—even if the other applications have their Background option selected. The advantage of this option is that the application controlled by this PIF will run faster and have access to more memory.

- *Close Window on Exit* directs Windows to close the application's window when the application ends, as opposed to displaying the application's ending screen and prompting you with the message Hit Any Key To Exit.

At the bottom of the dialog box is a button labeled Advanced. Choosing Advanced brings up a second dialog box, similar to the one in Figure 4-33.

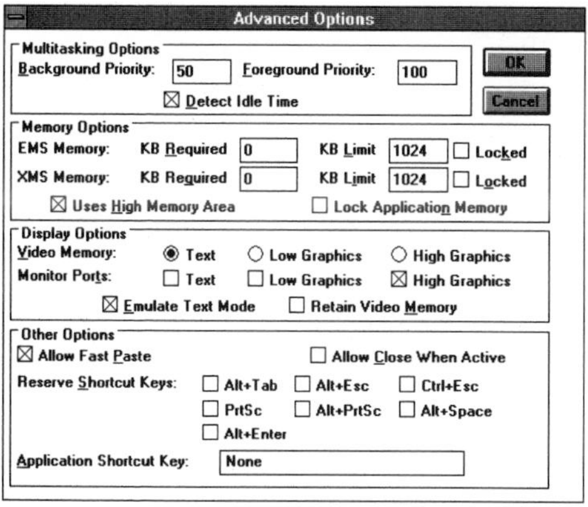

FIGURE 4-33. *The Advanced Options dialog box.*

The following paragraphs briefly describe the fields in this dialog box:

■ *Background Priority* and *Foreground Priority* control the amount of time Windows spends running the application when the application is running in the background or in the foreground. Priority values range from 0 to 10,000. These values are meaningful only when compared to other applications.

For example, suppose three applications are running. The application in the foreground has a foreground priority of 100, and the two applications in the background have a background priority of 50. Therefore, the total priority for all applications is 200. Windows spends a percentage of time running each application equal to the applications priority divided by the total priority of all applications. Therefore, the foreground application is running 50 percent of the time (100 ÷ 200), and each background application is running 25 percent of the time (50 ÷ 200).

- *Detect Idle Time* directs Windows to let other applications run while an application is idle, waiting for your input.

- *EMS Memory* has three options: KB Required, KB Limit, and Locked. KB Required tells Windows the minimum amount of expanded memory the application needs. KB Limit is the maximum amount of expanded memory Windows lets the application use. Selecting the Locked check box prevents Windows from swapping the contents of the application's expanded memory to disk. This increases the application's performance but decreases overall Windows performance.

- *XMS Memory* has three options: KB Required, KB Limit, and Locked. KB Required tells Windows the minimum amount of extended memory the application needs. KB Limit is the maximum amount of extended memory Windows lets the application use. Locked prevents Windows from swapping the contents of the application's extended memory to disk. This increases the application's performance but decreases overall Windows performance.

- *Uses High Memory Area* tells Windows that the application can use the high memory area (the first 64 KB of extended memory).

- *Lock Application Memory* prevents Windows from swapping the program to disk. This increases the application's performance but decreases overall Windows performance.

- *Video Memory* specifies how much memory Windows must reserve to save the application's window when it changes between tasks. If the application uses text mode, select Text. If the application uses CGA graphics, select Low Graphics. If the application uses EGA or VGA graphics, select High Graphics.

- The *Monitor Ports* check boxes help prevent problems that can occur when an application directly interacts with your computer's display adaptor. If your application's display looks normal, don't modify these settings because they slow down the application significantly. Otherwise, select the option button that corresponds to the video mode the application runs in (Text for text mode, Low Graphics for CGA graphics mode, and High Graphics for EGA or VGA graphics mode).

■ *Emulate Text Mode* lets Windows quickly display an application's text output. Leave this option selected unless the application's display doesn't appear properly.

■ *Retain Video Memory* directs Windows not to reduce the amount of memory used for an application's display when the application is running. This prevents the application from losing video memory when you switch to another application.

■ *Allow Fast Paste* lets Windows paste text from the clipboard into the application as fast as possible. If an application has difficulties with paste operations, disable this option.

■ *Reserve Shortcut Keys* directs Windows to reserve the specified key combinations for use by the application instead of treating the key combinations as predefined Windows keyboard combinations.

■ *Application Shortcut Key* lets you specify a keyboard combination that makes the application the foreground task.

Installing Windows

If you need to install Windows, this section will help you do so. Note that before you can continue, you must be using DOS version 3.1 or later.

WINDOWS HARDWARE REQUIREMENTS

To use Windows, you need

- An IBM-compatible computer with an 8088, 8086, 80286, 80386, 80386SX, i486, i486SX, or compatible microprocessor

- 640 KB of memory (384 KB of extended memory recommended)

- A hard disk with 6 to 8 MB (or more) of available storage

- A CGA, EGA, VGA, 8514/A, or Hercules graphics adapter and monitor (EGA or higher recommended)

- A mouse (not necessary, but highly recommended)

Installing Windows

Before you begin the Windows installation, note your computer's video adapter, mouse, printer type, and the port your printer plugs into (typically LPT1 for parallel printers and COM1 for serial printers). If your computer connects to a network, note the network's name and version number.

Place Windows floppy disk 1 in drive A, and use the following command to change to drive A:

```
C:\>a: <Enter>
```

Then use the following command to run Setup:

```
A:\>setup <Enter>
```

You'll see information about the Windows installation. Read the information, and press Enter to continue.

A screen will prompt you to name the directory in which Windows should be installed. (The default is C:\WINDOWS.) Press Enter to select this directory.

A System Information screen will list the equipment in your computer. If the list is accurate, press Enter. If you need to make corrections to the list, follow these steps:

1. Use your keyboard arrow keys to highlight the incorrect item, and then press Enter. You'll see a list of alternatives.

2. Use the arrow keys to highlight the correct item, and then press Enter to return to the System Information screen.

3. When all items shown in the System Information screen are correct, press Enter.

Setup begins copying files to your hard disk. From time to time, as the installation continues, Setup asks you to insert a particular Windows disk. Insert the disk that Setup needs, and then press Enter to continue.

Eventually, you'll see the dialog box shown in Figure A-1. Press Enter to continue.

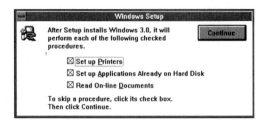

FIGURE A-1. *The Windows Setup dialog box.*

Setup continues copying files from the installation disk to your hard disk, asking for various installation disks as needed. When a dialog box asks whether you want Setup to automatically update your AUTOEXEC.BAT and CONFIG.SYS files, press Enter. You'll see a dialog box telling you that Setup has renamed your original AUTOEXEC.BAT and CONFIG.SYS files as AUTOEXEC.OLD and CONFIG.OLD. Press Enter to continue.

Selecting a Printer

Printer selection is actually a two-step process: First you select a printer you intend to use, and then you configure it. You repeat this process for each printer. The following sections describe this process.

Selecting a printer You'll see the dialog box shown in Figure A-2, requesting that you select a printer.

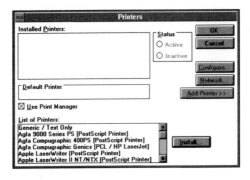

FIGURE A-2. *The Printers dialog box.*

1. Use the arrow keys to scroll through the printer list and highlight your printer. (To speed up this process, type the first letter of your printer's name.) If your printer's name does not appear, highlight Unlisted Printer.

2. Press Enter.

3. Setup will ask you to insert another disk. Do so and press Enter. Repeat steps 1 and 2 if you have multiple printers.

Configuring a printer Setup assumes that your printer attaches to the parallel port LPT1. If your printer is attached to a different port, follow these steps:

1. Select the printer in the Installed Printers: list box, and then hold down the Alt key and press C. You'll see the dialog box shown in Figure A-3.

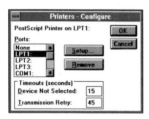

FIGURE A-3. *The Printers-Configure dialog box.*

2. Use your arrow keys to highlight the correct port, and then press Enter.

Setting Up Applications

After you select and configure each of your printers, press Enter. You'll see a dialog box similar to the one shown in Figure A-4.

FIGURE A-4. *The Set Up Applications dialog box.*

Windows needs to be informed of your existing DOS applications if you intend to run them from the Windows environment. An easy way to do this is to let Setup search all your hard disks for existing applications. Press Enter to do this.

When the search is complete, you'll see a dialog box similar to the one shown in Figure A-5.

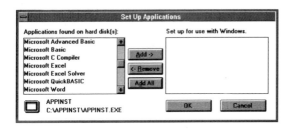

FIGURE A-5. *The expanded Set Up Applications dialog box.*

You can add all applications, or you can add individual applications, as described in the following sections.

Adding all applications To add all applications, hold down the Alt key and press D. Then choose OK to add them to Windows.

Adding individual applications To add individual applications to Windows, follow these steps:

1. Use the arrow keys to highlight the application, and then press the Spacebar.

2. Hold down the Alt key and press A.

3. Repeat steps 1 and 2 for each application you want to add to Windows. When your list of applications is complete, choose OK to add them to Windows.

Removing an Application

To remove an application, follow these steps:

1. Press the Tab key to move the cursor to the Set up for use with Windows list box.

2. Use the arrow keys to highlight the application, and then press the Spacebar.

3. Hold down the Alt key and press R.

4. Repeat steps 1 and 2 for each application you want to remove. Then press OK.

Reading the README.TXT File

Next you'll see Notepad (discussed in Part IV) and the README.TXT file. README.TXT contains important

Windows documentation that you should take time to look through. Use the arrow and the PgUp/PgDn keys to scroll through the file's contents, or—better yet—print the file by following these steps:

1. Hold down the Alt key and press F. Next press P.

2. Hold down the Alt key and press F. Next press X to exit Notepad and continue the installation.

Completing the Installation

When you exit Notepad, you'll see the dialog box shown in Figure A-6, which indicates that installation is complete.

FIGURE A-6. *The Exit Windows Setup dialog box.*

Remove the floppy disk from drive A, hold down the Alt key, and press W to start Windows.

Which Windows Mode Is Right for You?

Windows runs in one of three modes: real, standard, or 386 enhanced mode. The mode is dictated by your computer type and the amount of memory your computer contains. The following table describes the minimum CPU and memory requirements for each Windows operating mode:

Mode	CPU	Memory
Real	8088, 8086	640 KB
Standard	80286	1 MB (640 KB conventional, 384 KB extended)
386 Enhanced	80386SX, 80386, i486SX, i486	2 MB (640 KB conventional, 1 MB extended)

Each mode provides Windows with a certain degree of power. The following paragraphs provide a brief description of each mode and its capabilities.

Real Mode

Real mode is Windows' least powerful mode of operation. Windows automatically runs in real mode on computers that use the Intel 8088/8086 microprocessor (or an equivalent microprocessor) and on computers with less than 1 MB of memory. Real mode lets you run pre-version 3.0 Windows applications.

Standard Mode

Windows automatically runs in standard mode on computers that use the Intel 80286 microprocessor (or an equivalent microprocessor) and have 640 KB of conventional memory and at least 384 KB of extended memory. Standard mode lets you start and run as many Windows applications as you'd like, limited by the amount of available memory. You can run non-Windows applications as well, but non-Windows applications must use the full screen and run in the foreground only.

386 Enhanced Mode

386 enhanced mode is Windows' most powerful operating mode. Windows automatically runs in 386 enhanced mode on computers with an 80386SX, 80386, i486SX, or i486 microprocessor with 640 KB of conventional memory and at least 1 MB of extended memory.

In 386 enhanced mode, Windows can treat free space on your hard drive as extra memory. (This is known as virtual memory.) In 386 enhanced mode, you can start and run as many Windows applications as you'd like, limited by the amount of available memory. 386 enhanced mode also lets non-Windows applications run in the full screen or in a window.

Windows and DOS Initialization Files

Windows uses two initialization files: WIN.INI and SYSTEM.INI. The WIN.INI file stores information on how you've customized Windows; SYSTEM.INI contains information about your computer's hardware. DOS also uses two special files: AUTOEXEC.BAT and CONFIG.SYS. AUTOEXEC.BAT contains commands that you want DOS to execute every time your computer boots, and CONFIG.SYS contains commands that configure DOS for your computer. This appendix describes how to set up these files to best advantage.

Using WIN.INI

Along with customization information, WIN.INI contains two lines that automatically run applications when Windows starts. These are the LOAD= and the RUN= lines. Both automatically start the applications you list, but LOAD minimizes an application to an icon, whereas RUN runs an application in a window.

To have Windows automatically run an application, use a text editor (such as Notepad, which is described in Section IV) to edit WIN.INI, and place the name of the application after the equal sign on either the LOAD= or RUN= line. You can list multiple applications—simply separate their names with a space.

NOTE: *Leave the other lines in WIN.INI alone. Improper modifications to them could cause problems for Windows.*

For example, to have Windows automatically load the Clock and Notepad applications when the system starts, you would create a WIN.INI LOAD= line that looked like this:

```
LOAD=CLOCK.EXE NOTEPAD.EXE
```

NOTE: *If an application is not in your computer's search path, you must specify the full pathname to the application.*

Using SYSTEM.INI

The SYSTEM.INI file contains hardware-specific information—for example, information about your display, keyboard, and network. In general, the best way to change settings in SYSTEM.INI is through the Setup application or through the Control Panel applications.

NOTE: *If you are experiencing hardware incompatibilities, print the SYSINI.TXT, SYSINI2.TXT, and SYSINI3.TXT files. These files provide a detailed explanation of each line in SYSTEM.INI, along with recommended settings.*

Using AUTOEXEC.BAT

If you create a RAM disk for temporary files, you should assign the TEMP environment variable to it. To do so, place the following command in your AUTOEXEC.BAT file. (X represents the drive letter of the RAM disk.)

```
SET TEMP=X:
```

Starting Windows Automatically

To have Windows run automatically when you turn your computer on, place the WIN command at the end of your AUTOEXEC.BAT file.

Using CONFIG.SYS

Depending on what hardware your computer uses, your CONFIG.SYS file might need to install one or more of the following device drivers:

Driver	What It Does
HIMEM.SYS	Provides 80286-based, 80386SX-based, 80386-based, i486SX-based, and i486-based computers with extended memory support
SMARTDRV.SYS	Creates a disk cache, which improves computer performance
RAMDRIVE.SYS	Creates a RAM disk
EMM386.EXE	Lets 80386SX-based, 80386-based, i486SX-based, and i486-based computers simulate expanded memory using extended memory
EGA.SYS	Lets Windows work with EGA video cards
MOUSE.SYS	Lets Windows work with a mouse

NOTE: *The version of EMM386 that comes with Windows is called EMM386.SYS. The version that comes with DOS 5 is called EMM386.EXE. Use EMM386.EXE if you use DOS 5; otherwise use EMM386.SYS.*

APPENDIX C

Fundamental Window Keys

In Windows 3 you can perform a number of tasks with a few simple key combinations. The first of the following tables lists the key combinations typically used within a window. The second table lists key combinations commonly used within a dialog box.

Key(s)	Function
Alt+Space	Opens an application window's Control menu
Alt+Hyphen	Opens a document window's Control menu
Alt+F4	Closes the active window
Alt+Esc	Selects the next window or icon
Alt+Tab	Activates the next application window, restoring icons
Alt+PrtSc	Copies an image of the active window to the clipboard
Ctrl+Esc	Selects the Task List
Ctrl+Tab	Activates the next document window
Ctrl+F4	Closes the active document window
Shift+F1	Activates help on a specific command or screen element
F1	Activates Windows' online help
PrtSc	Copies the current screen image to the clipboard

FIGURE C-1. *Fundamental key combinations used in Windows.*

Key(s)	Function
Alt+*letter*	Selects the element noted by *letter* (which is underlined on screen)
Alt+Down arrow	Opens the selected drop-down list
Alt+Up arrow	Selects an item in a drop-down list
Alt+F4 or Esc	Cancels a dialog box
Ctrl+/	Selects all items in a list box
Ctrl+\	Cancels all items in a list box
Shift+Up arrow	Extends the list-box highlight upward
Shift+Down arrow	Extends the list-box highlight downward
Shift+Tab	Moves to the previous field
Shift+Home	Extends the text-box highlight to the first character or to the first item in a list box
Shift+End	Extends the text-box highlight to the last character or to the last item in a list box
Tab	Moves to the next field
Home	Moves to the top item in a list box or the first character in a text box
End	Moves to the last item in a list box or the last character in a text box
Enter	Executes a command
Space	Selects or cancels a check box item

FIGURE C-2. *Fundamental key combinations used in dialog boxes.*

Index

Special Characters

* (asterisk), 30, 39
+ (plus sign), 29–30
− (minus sign), 30
? (question mark) wildcard, 39
286 computers, 77
386 computers
  enhanced mode options,
    74–76
  memory and, 77
  mode choice for, 152–53
  PIF requirements, 141–45
486 computers, 74–76, 77
8086 and 8088
    microprocessors, 77

A

About command, 46
accessories. *See* desktop
    applications
Accessories group, 22
addition, 87
Airbrush tool, 109, 113
alarm control, 94–95
Always Alert command, 52
Always Warn option, 75
Analog command, 101
angles, calculations involving,
    88–91
applications
  arranging icons, 27–28
  associating files with, 37, 38
  changing descriptions, 27
  desktop (*see* desktop
    applications)

applications, *continued*
  groups (*see* groups)
  moving between, 53
  non-Windows
    adding, 81–82
    Calendar and, 95
    multitasking with Windows
      applications, 74–76
    PIFs and (*see* PIFs)
    setting up, 150–51
  opening, 3
  running, 32–33
  sharing time in 386
      enhanced mode, 74–76
  sharing time with printing,
      51
application windows, 1
appointment calendar, 91–96
Archive attribute, 42
arithmetic, 86–91
Arrange Icons command, 27
ASCII files, 123
Associate command, 37, 38
asterisk (*), 30, 39
Auto Arrange option, 27–28
AUTOEXEC.BAT file, 149,
    155, 156–57

B

background patterns, 63–65
background printing, 48–52
background window, 76, 144
backing up files, 42, 104
Bad command or filename
    message, 1
batch files, 102–7

Kris Jamsa

Kris Jamsa graduated from the United States Air Force
Academy in 1983 with a degree in computer science. After
graduation, he moved to Las Vegas, Nevada, where he
began work as a VAX/VMS system manager for the U.S.
Air Force. In 1986, Jamsa received a master's degree in
computer science, with an emphasis on operating systems,
from the University of Nevada at Las Vegas. He then taught
computer science for one year at National University in San
Diego, California, before leaving the Air Force in 1988 to
begin writing full-time. He is the author of more than a
dozen books on DOS, OS/2, Windows, hard-disk manage-
ment, and the Pascal and C programming languages. Titles
from Microsoft Press include *Microsoft C: Secrets, Shortcuts, and Solutions; Microsoft QuickPascal Programming;*
and numerous quick reference guides. Jamsa currently
resides in Las Vegas with his wife and their two daughters.

The manuscript for this book was prepared and submitted to Microsoft Press in electronic form. Text files were processed and formatted using Microsoft Word.

Principal word processor: Debbie Kem
Principal proofreader: Deborah Long
Principal typographer: Lisa G. Iversen
Interior text designer: Kim Eggleston
Cover designer: Celeste Design
Cover color separator: Color Control

Text composition by Microsoft Press in Times Roman, with display type in Futura Heavy, using the Magna composition system and the Linotronic 300 laser imagesetter.

Printed on recycled paper stock.

In-depth Windows™ 3 Resources from Microsoft Press

RUNNING WINDOWS,™ 2nd ed.
Craig Stinson and Nancy Andrews
Build your confidence and enhance your productivity with the Microsoft Windows environment—quickly and easily—using this hands-on introduction. This Microsoft-authorized edition is completely updated and expanded to cover all the exciting features of version 3. You'll find a successful combination of step-by-step tutorials, helpful screen illustrations, and real-world examples that will help you

- expertly maneuver through the Windows environment
- quickly master each Windows built-in desktop accessory
- tailor the Windows environment to suit your work habits
- use Windows on a network
- master the rich features of Windows' built-in word processing, communications, and graphics applications
- and much, much more

544 pages, softcover   7³/₄ x 9¹/₄ $27.95   Order Code RUWI2

WINDOWS™ 3 COMPANION
The Cobb Group: Lori L. Lorenz and R. Michael O'Mara
This up-to-date resource thoroughly covers Windows version 3—everything from installing and starting Windows to using all its built-in applications and desktop accessories. Novices will value the book for its step-by-step tutorials and great examples; more experienced users will turn to it again and again for its expert advice, unique tips, and useful information. The authors also detail the features and use of Windows' Program Manager, File Manager, and Print Manager so that you'll be able to move smoothly and efficiently through Windows, control the environment, and easily manage files, disks, and printers. This volume contains a special eight-page section—printed in full color—that highlights Windows' exciting capabilities.

544 pages, softcover   7³/₄ x 9¹/₄ $27.95   Order Code WI3CO

TOOLBOOK® COMPANION
Joseph R. Pierce
TOOLBOOK COMPANION is the first and definitive book on using and understanding ToolBook—the software construction set that makes it possible for users to "desktop program" in Windows 3. This authoritative tutorial is for anyone—regardless of Windows programming experience—who wants to create Windows applications with ToolBook. Along with step-by-step instructions are dozens of practical examples that show how to create buttons, fields, and other elements in the typical Windows application. Also included is a special section on using OpenScript, ToolBook's built-in programming language.

720 pages, softcover   7³/₄ x 9¹/₄ $27.95   Order Code TOCO

The Best Books on DOS 5!

GETTING STARTED WITH MS-DOS®
AND THE *NEW* MS-DOS SHELL
Carl Townsend

This book is both a self-paced introduction to the basic features of DOS and a comprehensive user's guide to the MS-DOS Shell—the graphical user interface that offers intuitive point-and-click alternatives to hard-to-remember DOS commands and procedures. Includes step-by-step instructions for beginning to intermediate DOS users to carry out everyday tasks such as organizing files, running applications, and managing a hard disk.

208 pages, softcover   7³/₄ x 9¹/₄   **$17.95**   **Order Code GESTDO**

RUNNING MS-DOS,® 5th ed.
Van Wolverton

Now updated to include DOS 5, RUNNING MS-DOS, 5th ed., is the ideal book for all levels—from novices to advanced DOS users. For novices, this is a solid introduction to basic DOS concepts and applications. For seasoned users this book provides all you need to achieve DOS mastery—precise, real-world examples, thoughtful discussions, and understandable descriptions. The author addresses the exciting improvements in DOS 5 while providing in-depth coverage of every major version of DOS. Also included is a completely revised and updated command reference—an invaluable resource for *every* DOS user.

592 pages, softcover   7³/₄ x 9¹/₄   **$24.95**   **Order Code RUMS5**

SUPERCHARGING MS-DOS,® 3rd ed.
Van Wolverton and Dan Gookin

When you're ready for more—turn to SUPERCHARGING MS-DOS. This sequel to *Running MS-DOS* provides tips for intermediate to advanced business users on maximizing the power of DOS 5. You'll also find scores of new batch files and examples to help you get the most out of DOS. Move up to power user with this great resource!

425 pages, softcover   7³/₄ x 9¹/₄   **$24.95**   **Order Code SUMS3**

THE MICROSOFT® GUIDE TO MANAGING MEMORY WITH DOS 5
Dan Gookin

One of the most significant features of DOS 5 is its ability to use extended and expanded memory to effectively shatter the 640K barrier. This official guide provides clear information on how this is done. Beginning to intermediate DOS 5 users will find out how memory works and how to buy, install, and configure additional memory. Plus computer setup scenarios that demonstrate the options for maximizing memory. A great little book packed with advice.

208 pages, softcover   6 x 9   **$14.95**   **Order Code GUMAME**

Microsoft® Excel Books Mean Business

MICROSOFT® EXCEL STEP BY STEP
PC Edition for Windows™ 3
Microsoft Corporation

This is the official Microsoft Excel 3 courseware—the perfect training guide for business, classroom, and home use. Self-paced lessons, disk-based practice files, and real-world business examples provide you with the most effective and timesaving way to get up and running with Microsoft Excel 3. The lessons are progressive yet modular, so the novice can advance from one lesson to the next, and the intermediate user can step in at any point to learn specific skills. This method lets you get right to what you need to know. Become a spreadsheet expert the easy way, with MICROSOFT EXCEL STEP BY STEP.

304 pages, softcover with one 5¼-inch disk
7¾ x 9¼ $34.95 Order Code EX3STP

GETTING STARTED WITH MICROSOFT® EXCEL 3 FOR WINDOWS™
Ralph Soucie

If you've never used Microsoft Excel or any other spreadsheet before, GETTING STARTED WITH MICROSOFT EXCEL 3 FOR WINDOWS is the fastest and easiest way to master this popular program. This book is a straightforward, step-by-step guide and example-packed tutorial that is ideal for novice users. You'll quickly pick up the fundamentals of Microsoft Excel's worksheet, charting, database, and macro capabilities with this clear, concise guide. Includes dozens of timesaving tips, practical examples, and screen illustrations.

368 pages, softcover 7¾ x 9¼ $22.95 Order Code GESTEX

RUNNING MICROSOFT® EXCEL, 2nd ed.
The Complete Reference to Microsoft Excel for Version 3 for Windows™
The Cobb Group: Douglas Cobb, Judy Mynhier
with Craig Stinson and Chris Kinata

Here is the most complete and authoritative guide to Microsoft Excel available anywhere. It will give you a thorough understanding of Microsoft Excel in the shortest possible time. No matter what your level of expertise—seasoned spreadsheet user, beginning or occasional Microsoft Excel user, or longtime Lotus 1-2-3 user—RUNNING MICROSOFT EXCEL will be your primary source of information and advice. It's packed with step-by-step instruction, scores of examples and tips, and dozens of illustrations. The easy-to-follow tutorial style will help you quickly learn both the basics and most advanced features of Microsoft Excel including using the Solver to perform "what if" calculations, using the Toolbar to create charts and buttons, developing 3D charts, and much more. Learn how to use Microsoft Excel with other programs, file linking and sharing with Lotus 1-2-3, and using Microsoft Excel with Windows.

848 pages, softcover 7¾ x 9¼ $27.95 Order Code RUEX 2

Outstanding Word for Windows™ *References*

WORD FOR WINDOWS™ COMPANION
Mark W. Crane

WORD FOR WINDOWS COMPANION makes Word for Windows
easy to learn and use. Regardless of your level of expertise, you'll find a
wealth of useful information in this comprehensive resource. It's both an excep-
tional tutorial for new Word for Windows users and a master reference guide for
experienced users. You'll learn basic concepts of word processing, typography,
and design to create professional-looking documents with confidence and
ease. In addition to detailed explanations, the book offers scores of illustrations,
examples, and tips to enhance your productivity. An extensive index
and side-margin headings make information readily accessible.

896 pages, softcover $7^{3}/_{4}$ x $9^{1}/_{4}$ **$26.95   Order Code WOWICO**

WORKING WITH WORD FOR WINDOWS™
Russell Borland

WORKING WITH WORD FOR WINDOWS is the most comprehensive
book available for intermediate users of Microsoft Word for Windows. Written
by a member of the Word for Windows design team, this example-packed book
will be your primary reference to all the exciting document processing, desktop
publishing, and WYSIWYG features of Microsoft Word for Windows. In-depth
information, advice, and hands-on examples show you how to customize
the user interface, use a variety of fonts and type sizes, insert graphics into
documents, use macros to automate routine editing, position text and
graphics, link text and graphics within documents, and more.

656 pages, softcover $7^{3}/_{4}$ x $9^{1}/_{4}$ **$22.95   Order Code WOWOWI**